WINNING GRANTS

HOW TO WRITE WINNING GRANT PROPOSALS THAT
WILL GET YOU FUNDING FOR YOUR NONPROFIT

JAMES RUELL

CONTENTS

Introduction   9

STAGE 1: STEPPING INTO THE WORLD OF GRANTS

1. WHAT IS A GRANT, REALLY?   19
   What grants can do for you   22
   Types of grant proposals   26
   Chapter activity: Clarify your nonprofit's
   objectives   30

2. ARE GRANTS FOR ME?   33
   How do I decide whether to apply for a
   grant?   35
   When to apply for grants   40
   Chapter activity: Should I apply for
   grants?   42

3. LOOKING FOR THE MONEY   45
   Who gives grants? And why?   46
   Searching for grants and where to
   find them   54
   The grant application process   57
   Chapter activity: Figure out the right
   grant opportunities for you   61

4. GETTING INTO YOUR FUNDER'S
   SHOES   67
   What motivates grant-givers?   68
   Researching your funder and tailoring
   your grant application   70
   Engaging with potential funders   75
   Getting a funder involved in your project   79

After getting the grant: reporting back   80
Chapter activity: Investigate and narrow
down your leading prospects   83

STAGE 2: CRAFTING AN
IRRESISTIBLE GRANT APPLICATION

5. WRITING A WINNING GRANT   87
Getting the basics right   88
The 10 major parts of a grant proposal   89
Other supporting elements   118
More templates and samples to get you
started   121
Strategically positioning and pitching
your nonprofit   136
Chapter activity: Create your proposal
template   138

6. GETTING YOUR NONPROFIT TO
STAND OUT FROM THE REST   141
Tips to help your nonprofit stand out   142
Cross check everything against your
mission statement   147
Use your mission statement to ensure
alignment   150
The bottom line: selling your nonprofit's
story   151
Chapter activity: Put it all together and
customize to your top prospect   154

7. INSPIRATION FROM FUNDING
INNOVATION   157
Get innovative in your outreach   158
Ask for more than money   159
Present how you are learning and
improving   161
Go big   164

Further resources   166
Chapter activity: Write your cover letter
and executive summary   166

STAGE 3: REVIEWING YOUR
PROPOSAL FOR COMMON PITFALLS

8. WHY DO GRANT PROPOSALS GET
   REJECTED?   171
   Misaligned goals   172
   Your nonprofit did not seem ready for
   funding   173
   Non-measurable program objectives   174
   A weak budget   175
   Not following instructions to the letter   175
   A poorly written application   176
   Lack of credibility   177
   Chapter activity: Review your proposal
   and run it by your working group   181

9. YOUR CHECKLIST CHEAT SHEET   183
   Chapter activity: Clean it up, package it
   and hit send   187

   Final Thoughts   191
   References   195

HOW TO GET A FREE COPY OF THE ULTIMATE 4-WEEK FUNDRAISE WORKBOOK

Would you like a free copy of *The Ultimate 4-Week Fundraise Workbook?*
Get free and unlimited access to the below ebook and all of my future books by joining my Fan Base.

Scan with your camera to join!

"Donors don't give to institutions. They invest in ideas and people in whom they believe."

— G.T. SMITH (PAST PRESIDENT, CHAPMAN UNIVERSITY)

INTRODUCTION

You might *think* they care —but they don't.

The truth is, it doesn't matter how worthy your vision is. The real reason most grant proposals never make it anywhere is that your mission simply doesn't align with the goals of the organization holding the purse strings. If you cannot effectively connect the dots for the potential funder reading your application, then you are essentially condemning it to disappear into a black hole of doom. The proposal you've pored and sweated over; poured your heart and soul into is all for nothing.

Your nonprofit changes lives. You know the difference it makes for those you serve. You know the potential impact you could make with even more resources to draw on. You know you need to raise more money and create more predictable funding streams, yet it feels like there is a mysterious code to crack here that you just haven't figured out. Maybe you've sent out application after application but aren't getting hits. You might even have a sneaky suspicion that something is lacking in your written proposals, but you don't really know what it is. You dread sitting down to write; it is a struggle to sell your mission and trying to do so feels so unnatural. Perhaps rejection after rejection has you thoroughly down in the dumps and reluctant to try again. The prospect just feels too daunting to tackle. You have hit a plateau.

But what if it didn't have to be that way?

Imagine having a steady pipeline of opportunities you feel confident about—a seamless process for identifying potential grants and effortlessly writing applications that hit the mark. Once you understand where to find grants and the processes that sit behind them, you will see exactly what you need to succeed. Imagine being able to sell yourself and your charity with conviction and clarity while standing out from the crowd. What if you could stop procrastinating on writing and instead produce winning proposals with ease? What difference would that make? Would you have the confidence to apply for the funding you never thought you could secure? How much more reach and impact could your organization have, and what new possibilities would open up to you? Imagine what it would be like to have more security for your staff and programs. When you have the tools and techniques you need, you will find a renewed sense of momentum and assurance in your own fundraising abilities.

It may not always appear to be the case, but the money is out there. The Foundation Center (2004) found that 35 percent of those surveyed funded 50 percent or more of the grant requests they received. Many even accepted and considered unsolicited proposals. You only need to look in the right places to start tapping into these opportunities.

This book will demystify the world of grants—a key element in most nonprofits' funding strategies. Most people take a scattergun approach to seeking grants, when in fact, what is called for is a structured process. You already have all the skills and talents to win. Now it is time to develop a strategy that you can rinse and repeat. I will show you exactly how to up your game and start consistently winning grants.

You will learn the basics of grants, how to find relevant funding opportunities, and the key stages of the application process. We will explore the why and how of putting yourself in a funder's shoes. This includes understanding their motivations, building relationships, researching their backgrounds, and then tailoring your proposal accordingly.

Then, we will get into the nitty-gritty of writing a winning grant. I will break down the elements of a grant proposal, explain each section in detail, and show how the parts all work together (complete with templates and samples to help you get started right now). We will explore how to position your pitch so you stand head and shoulders above the crowd, with ten practical tips to guide you in crafting a standout application. I will show you pitfalls to avoid based on the top reasons why funders commonly decline requests.

Your charity's goals may not be quantifiable by metrics such as sales or customers acquired, but it is still vital that you find a way to illustrate your impact to potential funders in a clear, measurable manner. They expect to see the impact of their grants and that the funds are being spent on the precise cause they were allocated to. It is up to you to integrate your insights and vision with facts, research, and numbers to convince them upfront and then to focus on performance measures and report back on outcomes in a timely fashion. Do not panic if you feel out of your depth here; this is the ground we will be covering in detail so that you are well prepared to back up your case.

Finally, winning a grant is not just about writing a convincing application. A key element of winning funding is credibility and trust. It is essential for any nonprofit to cultivate relationships based on trust, so we will cover ways to build credibility for your organization, raise its profile, and get wider coverage. Plus, we will look at thinking beyond conventional grant-giving and widening your horizon. No matter your experience level, and no matter the size of your nonprofit's budget, this book will equip you with the inside knowledge to write winning grant proposals over and over again.

I will guide you through, step by step, until you master what it takes to write a compelling story that makes it a no-brainer for funders to pledge their long-term support. You are going to learn how to make it easy for funders to say yes, so you can stop worrying about where every dollar will come from.

Leading a nonprofit comes with its own challenges, but the rewards are even bigger. For many years now, I have been the Vice-Treasurer and Board Director of an award-winning charity in East London. I have played a key role in applying for grants and improving our financial sustainability, and in that time, we have more than doubled in size as a result of winning several high-profile grants, taking on new service contracts with local government bodies, and expanding the management team.

My background in finance (honed at a trading desk within an investment bank) serves me well when it comes to responsibilities such as monitoring the charity's finances, creating finance and expense policies, and assisting with strategic decision-making. This deep involvement in the charity fundraising process has given me a front-row seat to what goes on behind the scenes. I know for sure that it is more than possible to build a sustainable source of income through grants with a systematic approach and a proven formula for writing proposals that clinch the deal.

Now I have taken everything I know and distilled it into the chapters ahead so that you too can start to raise more money and lay the groundwork for more predictable streams of income. The good news is, securing regular grants is a skill that can be learned. I will share insider tips on the art of writing proposals, common mistakes to avoid (this goes for both amateur and experienced grant writers), managing expectations in your proposals, and crafting compelling narratives that win your nonprofit the funding it deserves.

It all starts with getting the lay of the land: how grants actually work, where to find them, and the key types of proposals you need to get familiar with.

Ready to dive in? Let's get started.

STAGE 1: STEPPING INTO THE WORLD OF GRANTS

1

WHAT IS A GRANT, REALLY?

Let us start with the basics so that we are all on the same page. A grant is usually defined as a financial donation to a nonprofit organization for a specific purpose. That sum of money is intended to address a need or problem in a community. Most importantly, grants do not need to be paid back, making them an ideal source of funds for a nonprofit.

Institutions, either public or private, typically award grants, but the most common grant funding sources are government agencies (at local, regional, or national levels), corporations, and foundations. Individuals can also be grantmakers in their own right. Grants can range hugely in size and scale, from as little as a few hundred dollars to millions of dollars. Many are designed to fund specific work streams during a particular time frame, while others can be used to fund start up or operational costs.

Often, grants will be earmarked for specific purposes. For example, grantmakers generally focus on supporting a defined location (e.g., city or region), sector or population (e.g., migrants), or a specific type of nonprofit (e.g., educational). Grants may also be allotted to support a particular person, project, or program. In the private sector, grants are often targeted towards special interests based on the priorities of the donor, such as research into specific diseases or certain performing arts.

It is important to note that grants are not contracts. When you receive a grant, it is based on the understanding that you will use the money to have a go at accomplishing a specific objective that you have agreed to. While you would, of course, have reason to believe you will succeed, there is no guarantee. Failing to deliver would be disappointing, but there would be no legal consequences. On the other hand, a contract is a legally binding agreement. If contractual obligations are not met, there will be ramifications.

To apply for a grant, you would typically submit a written proposal to the entity behind it, outlining how you would use those funds and making the best case possible to support your application. That might sound like a time-consuming process, which it often is. Although it takes time and effort, the competition is often fierce, and you will have responsibilities and reporting requirements to juggle, it is well worth it to go through the process and win grants.

If you have been itching to launch a brand-new initiative (like starting a new program to fill a gap) or expand an existing project to meet growing needs but cannot cover those costs in your current budget, then grants might be the lifeline you need. There may be a funder somewhere out there with cash to spare that is designated for the exact type of service your nonprofit delivers.

There is plenty of money being disbursed through grants by governments, foundations, businesses, and individuals. Over 900 grant programs are offered by 26 federal grantmaking agencies in the US alone. It is not always easy to secure grants, but there is no shortage of availability. You just need to find the right match.

To give your organization the best shot at securing funds, it is essential to dedicate sufficient resources toward grant writing and take the time to customize each application. While a single proposal can literally take weeks of work to refine, an experienced writer applying for a combination of new and existing grants should have a 50-60% success rate. In 2019, 75% of grant seekers who submitted at least one proposal won an award. It pays to keep trying and hedge your bets; 94% percent of those who submitted three to five applications received at least one grant, and that number climbed to 98% among those who submitted six to ten grant applications (Submittable, 2020).

WHAT GRANTS CAN DO FOR YOU

Winning grants can have a significant positive impact on your nonprofit. Landing extra funding can obviously help you achieve long-term goals that would not otherwise be possible to accomplish. Plus, in the process of honing your proposal, you have the opportunity to reconsider those goals and refine what it will take to get there, as most applications will call for you to specify your organization's long-term objectives.

Applying for grants represents a chance for outside funders to get involved with your mission. As you tell the story of your cause and impact to date, spreading that message far and wide, you are likely to gain more support. It is a numbers game. The more exposed people are to your vision—the more who know about it —the better your odds of drumming up support and resources from surprising places.

Developing grant writing skills is a valuable asset for anyone in the non-profit sector. You will develop a thick skin and a sense of perseverance as a result. The process can be grueling, with months of waiting before any payoff, and you may often need to apply multiple times before striking it lucky. That said, it comes down to much more than just luck. In the chapters ahead, you will learn how to boost your chances of success, so you can improve your hit rate from the get-go.

Ultimately, funders are looking to support nonprofits they believe have a good chance of success. To earn their confidence through a written proposal, you will need to sharpen up your budgeting, planning, and organization as much as possible and show a high level of competence. Improving your organizational management is one of those things that is hard to find time for day-to-day. Impending grant deadlines can act as an impetus to prioritize these types of process improvement tasks.

Receiving a grant from a well-known institution, like a respected government agency or foundation, can seriously boost your nonprofit's reputation. That credibility can then help you secure even more funding from other sources in the future.

How many revenue streams does your nonprofit currently have? Diversification is essential for your organization's financial health. Any fundraising professional knows the importance of maintaining multiple streams of income to minimize risk and maximize sustainability. Grants can help provide diversification; once you know how to write and win proposals, this can become a dependable avenue of money, so you are not reliant on a single source of income.

Grants can also play a significant role in funding growth. If your nonprofit needs help to scale up, then a grant can offer the cash injection required for a large-scale initiative that you might otherwise struggle to fund. Landing substantial funding can mean the difference between launching a critical program or continually struggling to do it justice on a shoestring budget. Broadly speaking, grant funds can be used in several ways.

- **Program-specific grants**

Program-specific grants provide funding for a particular purpose, as outlined in your original proposal. Often, these only cover running costs and will not contribute toward administrative expenses.

- **General grants**

General operating support grants, conversely, can be used towards almost any type of overhead. However, these are less common and often hotly contested because they have fewer restrictions.

- **Capital support grants**

Capital support funding is usually directed toward significant activities such as constructing a building or similar large-scale expansion. For example, if building a new animal shelter is on your organizational roadmap, then this is the exact type of funding you are looking for.

- **Research grants**

Research grants are self-explanatory; they are designated for research and often linked to a specific individual researcher.

- **Non-monetary grants**

Finally, there are also in-kind or non-monetary grants. These provide support in other ways, such as pro bono services or equipment.

You will need to be crystal clear on the type of grant your nonprofit seeks as you embark on your funding journey. Understanding the main types of grant funding will help guide your efforts to concentrate on opportunities best suited to your needs and that you have the best chance to secure.

TYPES OF GRANT PROPOSALS

What comes to mind when you think of this phrase? For lots of people, it conjures up visions of thick, multi-page documents. However, this is not always required. There are, in fact, several different types of proposals in the world of grant applications, and the most appropriate format will vary based on the specific funder and the type of funding at stake. Let's now look at the main categories to better understand your best option depending on your particular scenario.

1. Letter of Inquiry (LOI)

A letter of inquiry serves as an introduction and is helpful to see if there is a match when you are first approaching a foundation for funding. Typically, an LOI runs two or three pages and provides a concise summary of your project. In any LOI, you should aim to describe the relevant need or gap, outline your plan to meet it, and specify how it fits with the funder's priorities. You might send multiple LOIs to different foundations to gauge any interest upfront and test the waters. Foundations will generally outline their preferences in guidelines that are readily available on their website. Be sure to follow any specifications they have given.

Most foundations prefer to receive an initial LOI rather than a full-blown grant proposal. Why invest lots of time if it turns out that there is not an excellent mutual fit? It is faster for an institution to evaluate a pitch based on a short letter rather than an elaborate package. They can quickly decide whether it makes the first cut and then request a more detailed application if it does. If not, then you can both move on. It also requires less effort on your part. An LOI can be put together in a relatively short time. However, that is no excuse to throw something together without giving it much thought. This is your chance to create a solid first impression; just think of it like an audition or an appetizer (instead of a full meal).

2. Letter Proposal

A letter proposal is more detailed than an LOI and asks explicitly for funds. If you are seeking sponsorship or funding from a business, many corporations prefer to receive a letter rather than a long formal proposal. In most cases, three to four pages will suffice. Your letter should describe your project, give some background on your non-profit organization, and include the amount of your monetary request or details of your sponsorship proposal.

Although a letter proposal is less work to create than a full proposal, there is a bit of an art to briefly communicating your goals in the right level of detail: enough that the receiver can assess your request, but not so much that it overwhelms them. As a guideline, give enough detail to go on but do not offer more than is strictly necessary.

3. Full Proposal

A complete proposal is what you probably think of when talking about applying for a grant. It is the most elaborate type of proposal and can range in length from just a few pages to around 25 pages at the top end of the scale, depending on how much information is required. The typical format for a full proposal includes:

- a cover letter
- a summary of your project

- the amount of money you are requesting to
  support the work

Please do not skimp on the cover letter; this is a micro-pitch in its own right and needs to pack a punch. Funders often set their own standards or guidelines for proposals. Read any directions carefully and be sure to follow the instructions. Many grants are now submitted through online application portals, so take the time to understand how these work. It can be wise to write your submission offline; then, upload each section individually.

Now that you know the ins and outs of grants and how they can help support your mission, let's answer the next question: are grants for me? Grants are available from a surprising number of sources and for all types of causes, but just because they are there does not mean that they are right for your nonprofit. Before exploring that, though, consider the following activity. Please note, all the activities in this book are designed to spur you into action and give you the best shot of raising funds through grants. I highly recommend you take your time with the activities, put some thought into them, and complete them all to the best of your ability. Before you know it you will have secured grant funding.

CHAPTER ACTIVITY: CLARIFY YOUR NONPROFIT'S OBJECTIVES

We have already established that applying for grants represents a chance for outside funders to get involved with your mission. There is no way you will get someone else to invest in your mission if you are not invested enough to communicate it to them clearly. Writing a grant will demand that you tell the story of your cause and impact to date, hoping to spread that message far and wide so that you can gain support. To begin toward that, make sure you clarify the objectives of your business. Some people start a nonprofit out of a general sense of wanting to change the world. Others have been personally impacted by a societal illness— like a disease, lack of access to resources, natural disaster, and so forth— and want to be part of the solution. Others still want to give their financial and emotional resources toward a cause. What is your reason?

Determine your motivating factor. It will help you to define your mission clearly and to outline your purpose as well as the programs you want. While doing this exercise, try to create a mission statement as well. Nothing has to be perfect, or complete, as of yet, but you just need to start. Consult with any others in your nonprofit and figure out if your objective and mission statement is true to what you actually do. If you already have a document with your objectives and mission statement, now is the time to test them and see if they are accurate. Ask yourself these questions:

- Why am I/did I start this nonprofit?
- What wrong am I trying to right?
- What values drive our programs and activities?
- Where will we accomplish our mission?
- Who is the target beneficiary group?

2

ARE GRANTS FOR ME?

In Chapter 1, we established that grants are wonderful. People give you money to do exactly what you love—sometimes what you have always longed to do. What could possibly cause you to hesitate to take such a deal? How many times in life does it happen? We established that grants:

- can give you significant funds with just one proposal
- give you money that you do not have to refund
- provide resources to do meaningful work
- come with prestige and boost your credibility and exposure
- can make it easier to raise money in the future because success births success

- can allow you to implement projects that would otherwise stall
- have no limit—you can apply for as many grants as you want every year

With such an impressive list of advantages, how do you determine whether a specific grant is a way to go for your nonprofit? Do you simply write a proposal because you heard that money is available? Think about this example for a moment: your group offers after-school programs for kids, and you are hoping to get more money for the programs. A local foundation provides funding for community groups like yours, but it primarily focuses on the elderly. To improve your chances of getting the award, you could create a program that involves senior citizens in your after-school programs, but should you?

A general answer to that question is "no." You should not do anything that will mean twisting your priorities, and definitely not if you have no interest in senior citizens. Perhaps if the new program design involving the elderly met your organization's needs, it might be feasible. Maybe you realize that it is an excellent idea you never thought of before. The question to answer in this chapter, otherwise phrased, is "how do I find a balance between staying true to my mission and yet not neglect other opportunities that come my way?"

HOW DO I DECIDE WHETHER TO APPLY FOR A GRANT?

This is not an easy question to answer, mainly because in the face of it, it appears like there are all reasons to apply for grants and none to support the opposite. For most people, the benefits of extra funding outweigh the drawbacks of the requirements connected with the financing. As you are probably aware, grants are not easy to get. First, you must know the suitable sources. Second, you have to write a proposal that knocks your target's socks off. These things take energy, time, and intense labor, and sometimes these labors are not rewarded because, let's face it, grants are competitive. Nevertheless, many people apply for them, for the same reason that you do. They consider the efforts they must use worth the fruit.

Of course, there is the fact that grant writing is learnable, which is the whole point of this book. You can learn to apply for grants and to do it well. You can develop the two main skill sets you need—the actual writing and the supporting activities accompanying grant writing. However, does grant writing fit with your organizational goals? As it is, nonprofits are barraged with funding opportunities, all having many requirements. Every funding opportunity is communicated through a request for proposals, applications, and similar guidance. Each has requirements for the prep and submitting of your application with detailed information about why the funding has been offered.

It is your job to review a solicitation document thoroughly and to analyze its specifics well before time so that you can pick opportunities that fit the predetermined criteria. If you are sending out many proposals, you can track the requirements in a grant management system to organize all the data you have to interact with. The process of deciding which of the many opportunities is the best for you should be systematic and well thought out to maximize your time and send out applications that match the resources and goals of the funder. Consider the following:

- **Does the project align with the funder's strategic plan?**

Every institution offering funding will have a strategic plan. Aligning your proposal to that plan is ideal from both their perspective and yours. Proposals that strongly correlate with the funder's strategic plan communicate that you will support the work and commit to completing it. The implication is that you do not need to apply for a grant if your goals and theirs do not match. As a rule of thumb, related strategic objectives will always be tied to the project's outcomes.

Funders want to invest in something that has a reasonable probability of success.

- **Do you have expertise and experience in the project area?**

Ask yourself: is this project that I am considering a new or weak area for our institution, or is it a strong area? Based on the funder's goals, this is something you must consider. For example, if it is a new area for you and the funder's goal is to begin a new program, you might be a good fit for each other. On the other hand, if the funder wants to offer mentorship to others based on the success of your project, it may be a red flag for proposal reviewers that an area is not your strong suit.

- **Who are the proposed leaders?**

Consider the capacity of the proposed project leaders. Are they people who are readily available in your institutions or institutions you partner with? Have they led similar projects in the past, and how did they do? Will they communicate capability to the person reviewing your proposal?

- **What is the financial potential of the grant?**

Will the grant, if awarded, give you a return on investment? Will the funding be enough to warrant the effort everyone puts into the project? Might it cost your institution more than the grant is worth?

- **Who might you potentially partner with?**

Collaborations and partnerships are an integral part of grant funding. Some funders like to work with nonprofits that are partnering for the expertise and sharing their results. In such cases, their solicitations will require support letters from partners. In addition, they will want to know how a partner contributes to the project's success—a component that will require planning and forethought. A grant funding opportunity with such requirements may not be for you if you cannot meet them.

- **Can you support the need from research?**

Sometimes, it takes research to convince a funder that the need you are trying to meet is legitimate. It could be that they come from circumstances worlds apart from yours. In such a case, think about supporting research that shows the need for your project. What is the problem, and what caused it? What activities support your efforts to solve it, and how will you evaluate them? If there is substantial data from third parties or reliable anecdotal information, you may stand a chance.

- **How competitive is the solicitation?**

Sometimes it is not worth it to go through the hassle of applying for a grant if there is a very low probability of success. Determine how many proposals are sent in response to the solicitation. How many projects were funded in similar cases in the past? Be sure to check the funder's website.

- **Do you have the capacity to respond effectively?**

Other times, you may be dissuaded from pursuing a grant because you do not have the time to prepare a competitive proposal. If you do not have the support of management staff to help with submission, formatting, and the likes, you may want to hit the brakes. While at it, think about all the resources you need. Are your people willing to commit to making them available?

- **Do you have a rapport with the funding institution?**

Think about your nonprofit's relationship with the funding agency. Have you had previous compliance incidents with the funder that could get in the way of success? Is the solicitation aimed at first-time applicants?

Applying for grant funding requires a lot of effort on your part. People working with and under you can significantly guide you to get financing that fits your overall goals. Putting these things to consideration can help you determine if a funding opportunity fits your resources and time.

WHEN TO APPLY FOR GRANTS

Before you can apply for a grant, you need to be clear about what reasons are driving you down that road. Take a step back and consider the large picture. Why exactly is a grant a good idea for your nonprofit? Ask yourself the following questions and think about your answers well:

- What truly are my long-term program goals with this move?

- Could I possibly do the same work well or nearly as well without the grant funding?
- If I get the funding, what exactly will I use the money for?
- Do I want to apply only because I know that the money is available?
- Is the grant the best way or the only way to do the things I want to do?
- Might there be other, possibly better, ways to get the money I need?
- Are my chances of success realistic, and am I clear about them?
- Am I ready to do the work to create a top-quality proposal for the grant?

If you have a team that you want to rally behind you, this is the point to have that conversation. Involve your stakeholders in that decision as far as is reasonable. Honest and careful answers to these questions will undoubtedly shape how you proceed and who you may involve in the grant writing process. That said, apply for a grant when:

- You want to begin a new project or expand an existing one, and you need money for that. Apply if you cannot cover these costs with your current budget.

- You know of an agency or institution offering grants that pay for the types of costs or needs you expect to meet.
- You meet all the eligibility criteria for the grants you are considering.
- You can commit the needed energy and time to the process of writing a grant.

CHAPTER ACTIVITY: SHOULD I APPLY FOR GRANTS?

Take some time to consider the things discussed in this chapter. Is a grant the best way forward for your nonprofit? Think about the types of support available. Might there be better financial options to pursue? While at it, consider the kind of support you would want. You may find that the type of funding you need will change, or you might decide to get help for your work through other means (see Chapter 7). Perhaps though, you will decide that you really want to write a grant proposal. If that is the case, you can more confidently move to the next step in your preparation.

Make sure you create a working group. From the people you have spoken to about your hopes, you have an idea of who would be most helpful in writing the proposal. Remember that often, you will need the input of others in planning the grant application. Even if they may not have expertise in grant writing, they may have attractive ideas for the content, helpful strategic thoughts, or specialized knowledge, which you may not have. Even if they lack these things, a working group can provide you with the support you need to do the job.

Ensure that the working group you create knows the way forward. Make them aware of the fact that you would appreciate their honest input throughout the whole process. Talk about what needs to go into the proposal and how to present it (more on this will be discussed later in the book). The group will help you for a short period unless you are submitting a very large application. After that, it need not help with the actual writing—just to share information, exchange ideas, gather data, and do the necessary legwork.

3

LOOKING FOR THE MONEY

N ow that you know the ins and outs of grants and how they can help support your mission, and you have decided they are the best funding option for you, let's turn to the next step: where to look for them. Grants are available from a surprising number of sources, and once you know exactly where to look, you might even find that you are spoiled for choice.

What is the first step for any successful grant writer? Setting their sights, of course. Before you even begin, you should dedicate some time to thoroughly researching the types of grants available for your nonprofit. However, if you are new to the grants game, it can feel overwhelming trying to pinpoint precisely the proper grant opportunities among all the options out there. This chapter is dedicated to the search stage: different ways to find funding and where specifically to look for relevant grants. I will walk you through the process of how to go about looking for grants and how the system broadly works, so you know what to expect.

There are grants designed for organizations at every step of the maturity scale, sector, and geographic region. Every proposal should begin with an audit of the landscape, so you can pinpoint all potential opportunities worth considering. Once you have done your homework, you should generate a shortlist, then narrow it down and pursue the most likely candidates.

WHO GIVES GRANTS? AND WHY?

In the world of funding, it is helpful to understand who is actually giving out money and why. Society is becoming increasingly complex, and donors' changing perceptions of giving reflect this. So, let's begin with a brief overview of various reasons why donors choose to fund grants or otherwise support non-profit work. For starters, you can win funds in the form of a large grant from a single donor. Donors give for many reasons. They may give out of a desire to change the world or give for personal fulfillment. Most wealthy donors are driven to make a difference in society and genuinely help other people. Tax benefits or ego boosts are a plus, but they are rarely the primary motivator. In the US, donor-advised funds are a fast-growing vehicle for charitable giving; donors make contributions when it suits them, receive an immediate tax deduction, and then recommend grants to their favorite charities. In 2019, donors recommended grants adding up to more than $25 billion to charities, according to the National Philanthropic Trust.

According to Fidelity (2016), donors are almost as likely to give because of an intrinsic motivator, such as personal values, as they give for an external reason, such as making a difference or meeting a great need. Although awareness of global issues is generally increasing, most donors believe solving domestic problems is most crucial. The challenges donors perceive as the most important societal issues to address for the future include:

- developing treatment or cures for diseases
- hunger and access to nutritious food
- access to basic health services
- protecting the environment
- access to basic education
- access to clean water

Individual awarding donors often fund causes that are deeply personal to them. These might be particular religious beliefs, political leanings, or sporting interests, for example. Someone who has close emotional ties to that organization or cause is more likely to support it regularly. For example, suppose you had lost several family members to a particular form of cancer. In that case, you might be more inclined to support a charity that funds research into the disease or provides practical support to those affected by it. Donors who have personally benefited from a service in the past or have a regular link to it because the issue is embedded into their daily lives are often driven to give back. They appreciate what they gained as a result of their experience.

Governments also give out grants. Various government agencies or departments often allocate these for specific causes such as housing, human services (e.g., for children or migrant communities), or education. It is essential for any nonprofit chasing government grants to carefully check whether their mission matches up to any government program.

It is worth noting that simply getting a government grant application ready to submit can be pretty labor-intensive. It may feel like there are never-ending hoops to jump through and the process is overly complicated. On top of that, short lead times are not uncommon. Once details are released, you may find that the deadline for submission is just weeks away. Conversely, the payout can be protracted, so the influx of cash may be slow to arrive. Government grants also tend to involve a fair degree of monitoring regarding how the funds are spent and whether they deliver the promised results.

On the plus side, many government grants are for hefty amounts and can mean a massive boost to your bottom line. In addition, government agencies often provide extra value to grant recipients, like assistance, consulting, or workshops, on top of the funding. Furthermore, they may come to consider your nonprofit as a leader in the field, giving you more influence when it comes to matters of public policy. Finally, being recognized as a recipient may open doors for introductions to even more potential partners or resources through the government networks.

Grants awarded by organizations often are geared toward solving big problems in the world. For example, Rotary Foundation aims to support projects in categories such as the environment, education, mothers and children, clean water, fighting disease, local economic development, and peace. At the other end of the scale, they might be focused on supporting local grassroots, community nonprofits. Corporate donations often look to fund projects or programs that align with their company values. Businesses are also often willing to donate goods that would otherwise go to waste, like perishables. By simply checking what causes a business supports or sponsors, you can get a good idea of what they believe in and are most likely to fund.

Here is a sample of the types of initiatives major corporates look to fund based on their gifting priorities.

- **3M**: 3M's corporate giving focuses on three distinct categories: education, community, and the environment.
- **Coca-Cola**: The Coca-Cola Foundation focuses on empowering women economically, health and wellbeing, and water—encompassing conservation and ensuring access to clean water.
- **Fidelity**: The Fidelity Foundation offers support in the form of substantial grants to larger nonprofits focusing on arts and culture, community development, social services, and health.

- **Ford**: The Ford Motor Company Fund provides grants to groups that focus on communities, education, and safety.
- **GE Foundation**: The GE Foundation's corporate grants are targeted primarily at health and education initiatives.
- **Goldman Sachs**: Through Goldman Sachs Gives, nonprofits that focus on education, communities, creating jobs, and helping veterans can all stand to benefit.
- **Intel**: The Intel Foundation is designed to support initiatives that advance science, technology, engineering, and math (STEM) education.
- **Nordstrom**: Most of Nordstrom's corporate grants are geared towards programs and organizations that prioritize and empower children and young adults.

Donors want to see the impact of their grants. According to The Guardian (2015), 58% of mainstream and 61% of high-income donors pay close attention to impact when choosing where to direct charitable funds. That is why it is so crucial that your organization's mission matches up with the funding sources you target. Today, the average donor is starting to more closely resemble an investor. That is, they are eager to get involved and to monitor returns and progress. Increasingly, they are willing to go beyond one-offs and engage for the long term. As modern funders are thinking differently, so too must the recipients of their money. This calls for a new approach to storytelling and evaluation. Kay Sprinkel Grace, author of *Fundraising Mistakes that Bedevil All Boards (and Staff Too)* and *Over Goal! What You Must Know to Excel at Fundraising Today* is credited as saying, "In good times and bad, we know that people give because you meet needs, not because you have needs." It is absolutely vital to get a handle on ways to effectively communicate the impact of your nonprofit's work if you want to maintain a high donor retention rate.

Donors today have more options regarding how and where to give, and they want to understand how their charitable dollars will be used instead of simply writing out a check and calling it a day. Consider the growing popularity of nonprofit measurement websites such as Charity Navigator and GuideStar. A Fidelity (2017) charitable study concluded that 81% of donors have questions or concerns about impact, ranging from unease about evaluating an organization's credibility to frustrations with those that do not always explain how a donation will be used. Further, two-thirds of donors say better understanding their impact would influence them to give more. Clearly, many donors struggle to get straightforward answers related to the impact of their giving. Most people understandably want to know whether they made the right choice in supporting a particular nonprofit or project. No one wants to help a doomed cause. If a program is thriving, then its supporters naturally want that winning streak to continue and will keep betting on its fortunes.

Keep in mind that many donors do not have a clear idea of what information they need. They just want assurance that their funds are going to the right place and being used well. According to Bridgespan (2011), past and current performance data, outside reviews from experts or testimonials, and feedback from beneficiaries are all perceived as valuable. They found that among the 700-plus foundation grantmakers surveyed, their top unmet need was an insight into nonprofit effectiveness. This group tends to consume relatively high volumes of performance information and is quite advanced in terms of what they expect to see, how they find this data, and how they use it to inform future decision-making.

However, precisely assessing impact is a tricky thing. Medical research can take years to pay off. Wicked problems like human rights and poverty may have no real endpoint in sight. So how do you measure societal change? In these cases, focusing on monitoring progress and quantifying benefits to individuals and communities may be the best option. Investors look for results at the company level. How do the numbers stack up compared to the previous year? But in the nonprofit field, donors must take a broader view. In considering impact, we often look at change at the community level—or even wider. Regional, national, and global organizations operate at an entirely different scale. The horizon is also longer. Businesses are incentivized on short-term performance, while nonprofits typically work to bring about sustainable, lasting changes.

Donors are entitled to clarity about the funds they bestow. They also need to be realistic about what can reasonably be tracked, how, and by whom. Nonprofits have a role to play in managing those expectations. Today, many nonprofits feel the pressure of donor expectations with different sets of reporting requirements for various stakeholders. Both donors and recipients should agree upfront on what kind of reporting can be provided and at whose cost.

SEARCHING FOR GRANTS AND WHERE TO FIND THEM

According to statistics compiled by the National Philanthropic Trust, giving is on the rise in the US, increasing steadily every year across individual, corporate, and foundation giving. In the UK, grant-giving by the top 300 foundations in 2017/2018 was £2.6 billion, accounting for about 90% of total independent foundation giving. There's still more good news on that front. In 2017, at least 18% of US public charities received a grant from a grantmaker. Candid (2020) analyzed all $10,000 or more grants awarded by 1,000 of the largest private and community foundations, representing about half of all foundation grantmaking dollars. The median grant amount was $35,000, and a quarter of the total funds were awarded for international purposes. The top areas that benefited included health, education, community and economic development, human services, and arts and culture. Funds were directed chiefly toward program development, general support, research and evaluation, policy reform and advocacy, and capacity building.

Where do you start? An excellent place to look for grants is on official websites, such as US-based grants.gov (join the mailing list for a regular roundup of current opportunities) or grantsonline.org.uk. Simply search for funding applicable to your nonprofit by category. Depending on where you are based, you might drill down to the regional government level. Next, explore local public agency websites to see what funds might be available. Choose departments that most closely align with your nonprofit's mission. For example, that might be the Department of Education, Department of Health, Family Services, Arts and Culture, Economic Development, or Transport. Then, spend some time strategically searching Google. You will want to have a list of keywords at hand that sum up the need you serve and the work you do. Consider sector, target audience or population, gender, race, ethnicity, physical location, etc. Brainstorm lots of synonyms to plug in, so you know you have covered as many bases as possible. Then, refine as you go depending on the results you get.

Here are some other sources to investigate, which may lead to even more resources as you hunt for relevant grants.

- Candid.org boasts a comprehensive directory of grants offered by private foundations, corporate foundations, and other charities that you can access with a subscription—along with many other free resources.
- At GrantStation.com you can sign up to receive opportunities by email or subscribe to access their members-only database which lists funders that accept LOIs freely.
- GrantWatch.com is a search engine designed to help universities, hospitals, government

agencies, schools, community or faith-based organizations, and research institutions find suitable grant opportunities.

- Instrumentl.com is home to a database of grants that you can browse by focus area or location, with full access reserved for members.
- TGCI.com, the website of The Grantsmanship Center, offers links to state-by-state funding resources, as well as a paid database of grant opportunities.

Think broadly when casting your net out. Who is giving to similar organizations? Where are your competitors getting their funding from? You may find fresh inspiration there. Also, consider asking your board members if they know of any grantmakers who potential candidates for financial support might be and, if so, whether they might be open to facilitating some introductions.

THE GRANT APPLICATION PROCESS

It is important to remember that every grant-giving organization will have different requirements. Pay attention to the details and follow any guidelines precisely as provided to give your nonprofit the best shot at success. Beware of any schemes that promise to help you land a grant in exchange for a fee. Unfortunately, online scams are rife, especially concerning government funding. That is a red flag if you are ever asked to hand over money to claim a free grant—this might be masquerading as a processing fee. Only go through official channels or websites. The typical grant process follows a general lifecycle, from the first announcement of the funding opportunity at stake, to implementation and review. The exact steps may vary from grant to grant; however, the broad strokes of the process are pretty universal.

1. Calling out for applications/proposal solicitations

The first stage begins with the grantmaker calling out for applications, advertising the opportunity, and inviting submissions. Then, as an applicant, you would review the criteria and determine your eligibility. If you tick all the boxes and decide to pursue the grant, the next step would usually be to register and create an account online. Then, you would complete an application, gathering supporting materials as required, before finally submitting a finalized proposal. Do not be fooled; this step can take days or weeks. You may be asked for information ranging from basic details about your nonprofit to in-depth explanations of the proposed project or program of work, along with financial data or other supporting content.

2. Initial screening

Once your proposal is submitted and the deadline for all submissions passes, the awarding agency will retrieve these and get to work. There may be an initial screening stage to ensure your application meets basic minimum requirements to qualify. For example, is the application complete with all fields filled out? Does your nonprofit or project meet all eligibility criteria for the grant? If not, it may be rejected at this early stage and proceed no further.

3. Full assessment and review

If your project passes muster, it will progress to a more thorough assessment of its actual contents. Each application will be reviewed and evaluated on the merits of program, technical, and financial perspectives; a cost analysis may factor in the amount you are requesting and how it matches up against the total pool of funds. How an institution chooses to conduct this review is up to them. However, a standard method is the panel approach in which a minimum of three people independently scores each application. They then reconvene to discuss their ratings in more detail. There will be policies to ensure all applicants are treated fairly and objectively and to eliminate any conflicts of interest among the reviewers. During this process, you may or may not receive updates on the status of your application as it progresses through internal stakeholder review.

4. Awarding the grant

The next phase covers the awarding of the grant itself. This tends to be the shortest stage in the process, usually lasting no more than a month or so. However, it is often an action-packed whirlwind. Once the review process is complete, successful applicants will be informed and congratulated. Recipients may be granted the total amount they requested or a partial sum. Next, the awarding organization will work with each recipient to finalize details and organize the release of funds. By this point, a significant amount of time could have passed, and things may have changed since you submitted your original application. If this affects your plans or timeline, now is the time to raise any issues. Otherwise, once you have reviewed your proposal, it is time to start planning for implementation with the disbursed money.

5. Implementation and closing the loop

The last stage of the grant life cycle is about implementation and closing the loop. This is usually the most prolonged phase and can even stretch out across multiple years, depending on the specifics of a particular grant. This is the time to send a personalized thank-you note. Then, with the grant payment now safely in your bank account, you can finally kick off that long-awaited project. It would help if you also started planning for impact evaluation in anticipation of reporting back further down the line. If you did not receive any guidelines regarding reporting expectations, ask about requirements; if they have no formal requirements, plan to send an update or two at critical milestones—sharing results, successes, challenges, and lessons learned. Stories and testimonials can also be nice touches to include. Schedule these to-dos in the calendar so it does not fall off your radar and be sure to add the funder to your mailing list. The final touch is wrapping up the administrative, financial, and program reporting side of things once the grant is entirely spent.

From there, you may embark on the whole cycle again once the next round of grants opens.

CHAPTER ACTIVITY: FIGURE OUT THE RIGHT GRANT OPPORTUNITIES FOR YOU

1. Clarify your objectives and create an impact statement

In chapter 1, you defined your nonprofit's objectives. At this stage, clarify those objectives and state them as clearly and precisely as you can. Use them to understand the work you do, explain it, and create an impact statement. At this point, your impact statement does not have to be perfect, but it must be clear. The idea is for you to have a full view of the work you do and how it affects your colleagues, employees, stakeholders, community, and the world at large. This understanding will help you when you are trying to figure out which grant opportunities to pursue.

To convince a donor to part with their money, you need to know your project inside out and demonstrate a passion for it. You must thoroughly understand the need or gap and successfully convey your ability to meet it. Your project or program should have been discussed and dissected, consulted on, and mapped out, with as many relevant stakeholders as possible. If you have any doubts at all, this will show through. If you are not crystal clear on whether or how the initiative will meet the needs it is designed to meet, then any potential funder will likely also struggle to see it, and consequently be less inclined to agree to funding. Grantors want to know why your project will achieve its objectives better than another comparable project would. They are interested in how you have developed it, why it has evolved the way it has, and who has had input into its design. If end users have been involved in helping to shape it, use this to your advantage to illustrate how well your nonprofit is tuned in to community needs.

2. Curate a list of institutions/foundations to target

Begin by visiting government websites. If you are in the US, visit Grants.gov. If in the UK, go to Grantsonline.org.uk. If you are in another country, find the equivalent government websites and interact with the opportunities posted there. Be sure to join their mailing list so that you can always keep updated on what is happening. From there, visit your local public agency websites and come up with a list of possible grants you could apply for. Then, perform a Google search (or use other search engines) using targeted keywords. Create your keywords by combining words that best describe the work you do and use those too in your search. The following table shows some examples of keywords and the organizations or projects they align with. Use it as a guide to create your own keywords.

Type of organization	Possible keywords
organization providing food and shelter for homeless people (women, children, and men)	child services, adults, youth services, economically disadvantaged, food distribution, homeless, housing/shelter, human services
organization delivering food to the elderly where they live	food distribution, food services, economically disadvantaged, disabled, elderly services, aging
organization educating children between 4 to 18 years old	youth development, children services, child development, education, youth services, education

Do not be afraid to cast your net wide as you create your list. Once you have a list of say 20 possible opportunities, make a list of the funder websites and the requirements you can find at first glance. Your question at this point will not just be "could they fund our work" but also "are they people I am willing to work with?" They will be reviewing your nonprofit at some point. This is the stage where you review their work. Specify, using your impact statement and objective/mission statement, eliminate the options that do not align with what you do to remain with at least ten possible options. To make your work easier later on, make a document with the opportunities you end up with specifying what they need from you. Do they need an LOI or letter proposal? What is their submission mode? Do they have an online portal, or do you mail your proposal to them? Be as thorough as you could possibly be.

4

GETTING INTO YOUR FUNDER'S SHOES

You are a bona fide expert in your field and know everything about your organization inside and out. You can talk about its mission for hours and spout off statistics and stories without even blinking. It is only natural, after all. That is what you do all day. This is what makes you great at what you do. It is what you are engrossed in constantly, and in the non-profit world, coming up for air is often a luxury. You know how to hustle and get things done.

But have you ever stopped to think about what it's like on the other side, from the perspective of a grant-giver? What goes through their minds? What are their hopes, priorities, worries, or concerns? If you can begin to think like a grantmaker, put yourself in their shoes, then you will have a better understanding of what they are looking for. That means you will be able to better tailor your proposals accordingly to hit all the right notes. In this chapter, you will learn to come at grant writing from the point of view of a funder. Armed with this new lens, you can then start to write more effective applications that win out against the competition.

WHAT MOTIVATES GRANT-GIVERS?

Understanding your funder is an important first step if you really want to give your nonprofit a leg up when pursuing grants. Gaining a broad appreciation of donor behavior and psychology is essential for anyone who wants to write grants well and to win them. When you know the types of causes a grantor prefers to support, you will be better placed to get their attention, artfully frame up your request in your application, and thank them appropriately. No matter the size of their charitable budget, small-scale donors and multi-millionaires alike start from the same place. Their philanthropy is about fulfilling a purpose, and that purpose can vary widely. When done right, giving at any end of the spectrum should be equally rewarding for the donor. Every single donor should feel valued, be confident that they know how their funds are being spent and know the difference they have helped to make.

Grabbing a donor's attention is the first step in gaining their support, which may then, with any luck, blossom into a long-term relationship. Donors might be initially attracted to a nonprofit through a particularly attention-grabbing campaign, for example, then get to know more about the organization's streams of work. To give money, they need to trust in your ability to deliver on your mission and have confidence that their donation will be used wisely. This is an essential step on their psychological journey from awareness to conversion. Their giving might not directly map to the specific work highlighted in the original campaign that first made them aware of your organization's existence. They also need to be satisfied with how they are treated as a supporter. Your first opportunity to thank them counts for a lot; do not waste it. Approach it from the perspective that you are embarking on a journey to achieve a big goal together, and they play an invaluable part in successfully turning that dream into reality.

Assistant professor Jen Shang, who specializes in the psychology of giving and bills herself as a philanthropic psychologist, has studied thousands of people to learn more about donor behavior. In an interview with the New York Times (2012), she explained that charities can use specific words in their fundraising material that boost people's inclination to act in response. For example, women on average gave 10 percent more when solicitations included words like kind, caring, compassionate, helpful, friendly, fair, hard-working, generous, and honest. In contrast, male donors were more moved by words such as strong, responsible, and loyal.

RESEARCHING YOUR FUNDER AND TAILORING YOUR GRANT APPLICATION

Demand for funding is always high and these days organizations are receiving more and more applications for grants. This makes it vitally important to do preliminary research. Focus your efforts on targeting the right funders so that you are not wasting time applying to the wrong sources. This will greatly improve your odds of success. Scour as much information as you can dig up on every prospect to help you determine just how close a match your organization will be. Remember, having aligned interests is the single most critical factor when it comes to finding grantors. Many grant applications are turned down for the fact that they simply do not tie in with the goals of the funder.

Are you seeking funding to launch a brand-new program? Are you looking for support to cover general operating costs? Are you hoping to raise capital? Determine the type of support you need. In these cases, your most likely bets will tend to be foundations or corporations with an interest in your sector or subject area. It is also worth exploring smaller foundations, which are often more inclined to fund a local initiative or nonprofit than a national institution would be. Look for other potential sources of grant funding in your specific geographic area. Some institutions focus on supporting their surrounding communities. Others may offer certain grants that are only awarded to applicants that operate in specific locations.

If you find some hot local prospects, do your best to track down a personal link. The stronger the connection, the better. Perhaps one of your board members or top donors has a contact at that foundation or business. Do not hesitate to ask for an introduction – this will give you a significant leg up if you can arrange a meeting to discuss your nonprofit's mission or needs and put feelers out to see if they might be interested in providing help.

Once you have a list of potential sources for grant funding, get to know more about each funder. Explore their websites and dig into annual reports, staff biographies, and any other material that is available to find. Pay attention to their latest guidelines, which may have been updated recently. If you have questions that you cannot find answers to, then do not hesitate to pick up the phone. The more information you can collate, the clearer a picture you can build of each grantor and their motivations. That means you will have a better idea of how to tailor your approach for each funder, using common language that is likely to resonate and ensuring your ask is for a reasonable amount considering the context you are both operating within.

Too many nonprofits fall into the trap of spotting a potential grant opportunity and then try to retrofit a project to suit the criteria. If you try to shoehorn an initiative into an ill-fitting grant proposal, it will be evident. You should always be working from something that currently exists. If you already have a project proposal at hand, you do not need to waste time searching for examples, statistics, or quotes. You simply need to extract the relevant parts and summarize them.

The fact is some problems are very complex. A grantor may be worried about your prospects for success and wonder if you are being realistic about what is achievable, particularly when taking into account the total funding pool available and the size of your request. When it comes to scope, do not set out to try and save everyone. You risk over-promising and under delivering. It is better to set sensible expectations and then outperform them. Be pragmatic. Rather than aiming to decrease unemployment rates in your city, get super specific. What elements of unemployment might you be able to impact? A small nonprofit probably will not be able to single-handedly claim success in reducing total unemployment for the population at large. But you may be able to get more local youth into training or employment, or help stay-at-home parents successfully re-enter the workforce. Be honest about the limitations of your organization and its size. Your ambitions for impact need to align with the reality of the scale you operate on. Funders need to believe you have a good grasp of the challenge, your capabilities, and your role in the wider system. They are looking for specifics, not generalizations; they want you to paint a picture of the before and after, so they can visualize the changes that will occur.

Your donor base is not a monolith. Not all of them are alike and no two are identical. Some are wealthy and others less well-off. Some give regularly, some sporadically. Some are busy building careers; others have made a name for themselves already. Some are retired, some are highly active in the charitable sector. Clearly, communicating with all your donors in the same way would be a losing strategy. To effectively convey appreciation and effectively engage them, you will need to personalize your direct communications.

Enter segmentation. Any good database or CRM will allow you to record details about individual contacts. If you can start to group donors into various categories based on what you already know about them, you can start to craft increasingly tailored messages. You can then deploy more personalized letters and applications that appeal specifically to that group's interests, needs, capacities, and motivations. While there are of course commonalities that will span the various versions, segmenting enables you to customize requests that are appropriate and meaningful for each recipient. For example, you can segment by criteria such as:

- relationship to your organization (e.g., volunteer, member, alumni, legacy donor)
- donation amount (e.g., donors above or below a certain threshold)
- recency of last donation (e.g., within the last quarter)
- type of giving (e.g., monthly, annual, bequest, for a particular fund or program)

If you know that someone is interested in specific kinds of projects or programs, show them how their donations have supported work in that particular area. Thank them for their help to date and outline plans for the year(s) ahead that could be achieved with their support. If you are applying for a grant from an institution that is a legacy donor, play up the history of your nonprofit and highlight the long-term impact on the community you serve. Report on how any previous funds were deployed and plans for the next grant.

ENGAGING WITH POTENTIAL FUNDERS

Winning a grant is not just about writing your application for funding. To really lay the groundwork for success, you should begin the process of engagement well beforehand, building relationships with the people who are the decision-makers and guardians of grant money. Some ideas are simply best outlined in person, and some funders struggle to get comfortable with a new idea otherwise. An existing relationship with the grantmaker will dramatically improve the odds of having your application accepted. This may be a new approach for you, if to date your efforts have mostly consisted of sending off cold applications to nameless, faceless grantors. If you have not done this type of thing before, then the information in this next section will be invaluable for you. Learn what to ask a potential donor and how to go about building relationships and establishing trust, so that when the time comes to make your ask, it's an easy and natural segue rather than a hard sell. Here are some best practices to follow:

1. Make preliminary timely contact

Not all grantmakers have the resources to have direct contact with nonprofit representatives. But among those that do, this is an opportunity to seize with both hands. Making preliminary contact is part of positioning your organization for a successful funding request. If anyone within your nonprofit has a connection with the funder, they should initiate the first approach. Otherwise, your chief executive may be best placed to lead the engagement effort. Sound things out within your existing network. If anyone you know has experience with the grantor in question, see if they are willing to dispense any insights and share any personal knowledge so you can get a better gauge of what to expect. In reaching out to corporates, institutions, or private donors, always remain professional. Plan ahead. Timing is important. Be cautious of reaching out before your project concept is sufficiently formed. If you engage too early, this can make it hard to speak to in any detail. On the other hand, leaving it too late can mean a wasted opportunity.

2. Explain the purpose of your visit and prepare

Make it clear that there is a purpose for your visit. In other words, let them know that you are interested in talking about your cause and any potential for them to be involved. That way, they will be able to ascertain who is best placed to meet with you and begin to formulate a response. Once you have made initial contact and your request for a one-to-one conversation is accepted, prepare thoroughly for the meeting. Plan how to structure the meeting—how long you will engage in small talk at the beginning and how to naturally transition into the ask itself. Do your research on the person you are meeting with. Do they have a history of giving? What concerns, fears, or objections might they have? What do they care about? What other causes do they support? Keep in mind that as an outsider, they may take more time to understand the basics of your organization than you might have expected. Your mission and needs may not be immediately clear to them. That means the critical question of eligibility—which is the main thing you are there to feel out—might not be easy to judge. If it's still unclear, do not hesitate to ask directly.

3. Practice, practice, practice

Practice every element of your ask. This is not the time to falter. To quote John D. Rockefeller: "Never think you need to apologize for asking someone to give to a worthy objective, any more than as though you were giving him an opportunity to participate in high-grade investment. Whether or not he should give to that particular enterprise, and if so, how much, it is for him alone to decide." By the time you are face to face, you should already have rehearsed the conversation many times over, playing out different possible scenarios. You should have your talking points memorized, know how to address common objections with grace, and finally shift gears into your request—which should be very specific and leave no room for misinterpretation.

4. Ask for feedback

Most people simply want to feel heard, so do not hesitate to ask for their impressions and input. Being asked for advice makes anyone feel important, and a potential donor is an especially valuable contact. One last word: do not read too much into these kinds of meetings. Do not mistake politeness or encouragement to apply as anything more than a courtesy. You may also consider feeding back directly to the grantmaker on the value of the meeting, whether or not you proceed with a formal bid for funding.

GETTING A FUNDER INVOLVED IN YOUR PROJECT

Ideally, your funders would be just as invested in your work as you are. That is unlikely to be the case, but you can still do your part to get them excited, keep the engagement levels high, and increase the odds that they will want to continue being involved over the long run. It bears repeating here that donors want to see the impact of their grants and that the funds are being spent on the exact program or cause for which they were given. Here is how to stay on the right side of quality reporting and regular updates.

First off, the grant money you were awarded came from somewhere. The grantor might have received it from donations, the government, corporations, or other charities. Just as you are accountable to your funders, they too need to report back to theirs and show that funds have been wisely used. They want to ensure they are achieving their own objectives. For example, if they aim to support animal welfare, they are entitled to check that the grants they award are doing so. They can then point to these as good examples of successful projects, which they might then use in their own marketing or PR activity.

Project evaluation is a key part of the nonprofit lifecycle. Evaluations help show funders whether your nonprofit is a good candidate for investment and that you are a solid bet. They are also useful for internal purposes. An evaluation can help you consider critically what turned out well, what did not, and what you might try differently the next time around. Try to involve as many stakeholders as possible in pulling together the report, so you can get an in-depth picture of the successes as well as the problems you faced along the way. Pose questions to yourselves such as:

- What were the benefits for those involved?
- What were the best parts and why?
- What issues cropped up along the way?
- What did we do to solve these problems?
- Did we make any changes along the way?
- Did the funding get spent exactly as planned?
- What might be done differently in the future?

AFTER GETTING THE GRANT: REPORTING BACK

The point of this section is to prepare you for once you get the money you have been eyeing. It is to make sure that you are just as efficient in interacting with the funder as you were before they gave you their money. The first step in reporting back is to clarify if there is a deadline for submission and if there is anything specific you need to include. Look back over your financial records and put together a summary showing that the grant funds were used to run the activities you said you would, including receipts if necessary. Grantors are looking for evidence that you spent the money on what you said you would spend it on.

Review what you pledged to do; do not stress if the reality did not turn out exactly as planned, as most funders understand that things change. For example, you might not have secured all the funding you hoped for, or you might have shifted gears to accommodate feedback from participants. Include a short description of the activities conducted, along with figures on how many people took part or were positively impacted. If there was a particular target group you sought to prior-itize, mention how many from that segment benefited. We rarely know in advance how things will turn out, so be upfront about any changes in the plan. Pivots can demonstrate agility and flexibility. Show how you made the most of things.

Explain how you collected feedback and information about how the project panned out. If you can include direct quotes or photos (make sure you get permission from people first) this can really bring a report to life. You can run a survey to elicit quotes or simply reach out directly to people and ask them what the project meant to them. Then, record their responses. If those quotes tie back into the program goals, even better. Finish off with a succinct wrap-up that ends on a positive note. State whether you achieved your original goals as per the proposal and how it matched up against the priorities of your funder. You can also mention the types of work you are considering doing next, which is crucial if you are hoping to apply for more funding from the same grantmaker in the future.

This brings us to the end of the first section in this book. By now, you should have the lay of the land when it comes to grants for nonprofits. You should be well equipped with a broad overview of the grants landscape: how they work, who awards them and why, how to find relevant opportunities, and what drives funders. Now it is time for the part you've probably been waiting for. Next, we will turn to the nuts and bolts of what makes a grant application stand out. What exactly goes into a proposal? I will walk you through the various parts of a typical grant and show you precisely how to write a winning grant application.

CHAPTER ACTIVITY: INVESTIGATE AND NARROW DOWN YOUR LEADING PROSPECTS

By this point, you have a list of many potential funding opportunities you could explore. What you need to do now is find out as much as you can about them, so that you can rule out some and prioritize the rest. By the end of this exercise, you want to have at least five opportunities whose requirements you meet well and that align with your project's goals and roadmaps. Work on your list, from the first one, downwards. Call the foundations where they have provided contact information. Where someone in your working group has connections, ask them to initiate contact and connect you. Ask for information where it has not been provided on the website. Interact with the application guidelines and the grants lists for the previous years. Who received money previously? What amounts? Do your homework thoroughly—it will save you a lot of trouble and time in the end.

As you do this, you will find that some opportunities no longer suit you while others will appear more suitable. Arrange them in descending order from the most desirable to the one that would be simply okay. For the rest of the exercises in this book, we will work on sending an application to the grant opportunity that you ranked first. You can later re-create the process for the other opportunities. Make sure you collaborate with your working group as you rule opportunities out and rank the rest.

STAGE 2: CRAFTING AN IRRESISTIBLE GRANT APPLICATION

5

WRITING A WINNING GRANT

Even the most seasoned grant writers still deal with writer's block from time to time. There is nothing quite as paralyzing as a blank page. You may know all the facts and statistics but putting them together into a compelling pitch is another story. The good news is, developing a winning grant proposal is not magic or rocket science. Once submitted, you cannot control everything that influences a grantmaker's decision. However, you give yourself the best chance of gaining approval upfront by clearly communicating your nonprofit mission, credibility, the need at stake, your plan to meet it, and your passion for the task at hand. Once you learn the basics of this particular type of writing, you will be able to use the same formula to replicate your success time and time again.

This chapter will provide everything you need to get started in the right direction, including an overview of all the individual parts that make up a grant proposal, an explanation of each element one by one, and templates and samples to get you started right away. I will dive deep into the nuances of writing each section so you can portray your nonprofit in the best possible light in your pitch for funding.

GETTING THE BASICS RIGHT

Before you put pen to paper or fingers to keyboard, keep in mind the golden rules of grant writing. First, you need to nail your letter of inquiry. You will recall that this is the standard introductory approach required when you first initiate contact. This reduces the workload for both parties. There is less for them to wade through, and you do not need to invest too much time and effort into a comprehensive proposal that may not get read. Writing an impactful LOI distills your pitch into a summary with an attached budget. This gives the foundation a chance to express interest and gives you a chance to get a sense of your odds of success plus any adjustments you might need to make to your approach.

When the time comes to write a complete application, success will hinge on your ability to write engaging proposals. That means presenting your solution clearly, laying out the issue, and explaining your plan to solve it. Focus on what you intend to do rather than belaboring the problem. An action-oriented perspective should also be complemented with a reasonable dose of positivity; this is not the place for a guilt trip. It is easy to get caught up in the doom and gloom of wicked problems. Rather than focusing on all the terrible effects of underfunding in this space, take the stance that your nonprofit is doing outstanding work and will continue to do so regardless. Gaining additional funding would simply enable you to do more, better, and faster. Frame it as an invitation to come along for the ride. Focus on making a clear connection between your proposed work and the specific criteria for each grant, ensuring you adhere to the guidelines. Finally, ensure you are writing in polished, professional, and succinct language. Avoid jargon, overly technical terms, and using too many metaphors.

THE 10 MAJOR PARTS OF A GRANT PROPOSAL

Let's talk about the parts of a structured grant application to get familiar with the various elements.

1. Cover letter

Your cover letter introduces your nonprofit and proposal to the person who will be making the crucial decisions. A cover letter should aim to describe your non-profit organization briefly and its mission. Broadly explain your plans and how the grant fits in connecting back to the funder's stated requirements and interests. Clearly state the positive impact your project will have and convey your passion for the proposed initiative. The biggest challenge is keeping the cover letter suitably brief.

Always remember that your cover letter serves as a condensed version of your proposal. It should run no more than two pages; a single page is fine, too. Keep your cover letter succinct and ensure you do not repeat what is already in your proposal. The aim here is to convey how well you understand the funder and their requirements as well as how your proposal supports their goals. If you've had previous discussions with the funder already, make sure to reference those conversations; if you have previously been the recipient of one of their grants, express appreciation for it.

A cover letter should include details on the nature of your organization, the need for your project or program, the target audience, an overview and benefits of the proposed activity, the amount you are requesting, and how this will help advance both your mission and theirs. Do not assume that this last point is obvious. It's up to you to explain why and to get them excited. Assume that the person reading your cover letter is entirely new to your mission and write as if this is the first time they are hearing about your nonprofit and the work it does. Build in one or two facts that strengthen the narrative you are telling. Keep all your paragraphs brief and focused. Every word needs to earn its place. Avoid falling back on jargon and abbreviations. It can help to ask an outsider, such as a friend or family member, to give it a once over.

Start with the contact person's name and title followed by the funder's name and address. In your greeting, address the individual using the right honorific. The first paragraph should start with an introduction to your nonprofit and the position you hold there. Then get to the point and state how much funding you are requesting and why your organization needs it. Briefly summarize what your organization does, backed up by a statistic or research-based point that speaks to the need being addressed. In your second paragraph, outline your organization's structure, history, and purpose. Then, describe why the project at hand is important and how it aligns with the funder's goals and priorities. Finally, finish your cover letter with a summarizing paragraph. Conclude with a final thought about the impact this funding partnership could have on the target audience for your project or program. It's important to sound thankful and optimistic in your closing, ending on a high note. For consistency, use the same date that you will be using on your full grant application.

Sample cover letter

Jane Smith

Program Officer

Blue Sky Community Foundation

123 Hill Rd

Central City

Dear Ms. Smith:

We are pleased to present this proposal for your review and look forward to partnering with your foundation to expand our after-school programs. ABC Youth currently provides tutoring services under the Study Buddy program, which aims to bring all participants up to grade level in reading, math, and science. Many students come from at-risk backgrounds and are testing up to two years behind their age group.

During the past three years, we have seen significant improvements among those enrolled, with most students improving their performance by one to two grade levels. Building on this success, we now seek to expand this service to address the needs of the growing Latino population in the area. Our proposal requests $25,000 in funding to support the rollout of the ABC Youth Latino Community Pilot Program. This would enable the procurement of new computers, training for tutors and facilitators, and a new van for drop-off services.

We appreciate Blue Sky Community Foundation taking an interest in helping our students.

Sincerely,

Sarah Green

Executive Director

ABC Youth

2. Executive summary

The executive summary is a brief overview of the proposal with more information about your nonprofit, your ability to complete the project, the need being met, methods to be used, and how those served will benefit. Based on this, a grant giver may or may not read the rest of the application, so it's crucial to make a compelling case here. It is the first thing the reader will see and needs to convince them that your proposal is vital to the community, that your nonprofit has the background and expertise to deliver it, and that your plan is relevant to their interests as a funder.

Also known as an abstract, the executive summary is designed to offer the reader a synopsis of the proposal. It needs to be concise yet highly informative. Aim for four to six paragraphs in length. One way to approach writing your executive summary is to consider it from this angle: *What is the essential question you are answering with this work?* Frame the need or problem as a succinct query, then shift into providing the answer through your proposed project or program. What do you intend to do? How will you do it? Why is this work so important? What has already been done? Provide a brief overview of the entire proposal, including the amount of grant funding you are requesting. It's often best to write this part last.

The reader needs to be able to take in this section at a glance. Typically, funders expect to see the name of the project, the main point person and their contact details, and a short description of the nonprofit. Outline your mission, specific competencies, the purpose of your programming, and long-term objectives with a nod to the mission of the funding agency. In relation to the specific project that your application is for, explain the exact problem being addressed, goals and objectives, a summary of the project, and expected results including how you will measure impact and define success. From a financial perspective, include the total estimated project cost, the amount of funds requested under the application, and any other funding sources.

Make the executive summary easy to read in terms of both language and formatting. Use headings for each section and bulleted lists as appropriate. Write clearly and concisely, so that the reader can quickly grasp your key points. Take a high-level view and describe the proposed project in broad strokes rather than getting too deep into the details. It might feel like you and the grantmaker are on opposing sides, with you vying for funding that they may or may not choose to dispense your way. Another way to think about it, however, is that you both share a common goal: being able to point to a completed project and claim a part in its success.

Sample executive summary

ABC Youth was established as a 501(c)(3) organization in 2012 by a group of former education professionals with a vision for a hub of activities and support services catering to young people across four suburbs. Our center serves more than 60 youths each day through our programs. Our mission is to help all youth maximize their potential through academics, sports, arts, and culture.

We are committed to adapting to meet the evolving needs of the changing demographics in our service area. Our Latino Community Pilot Project will provide access to academic and social services to youth in the growing Latino communities served by our hub.

Program objectives include increasing the number of Spanish-speaking youth who access our services for the first time within the grant period by 35%, engaging a minimum of 50 Latino families through our new parenting classes, and increasing the number of referrals of Latino youth from our partner agencies specifically serving this community by 40% within the grant period.

Our hub plays a vital role in the lives of local youth, as evidenced by our 97% approval rating last year. Our service area has a rapidly growing Latino population, which has nearly doubled in the past six years. Many of these families are at or below poverty levels and have English as a second language.

We believe that this pilot will introduce our hub and programs to an underserved population. As a result, we anticipate a rise in enrollments, increased diversity among those we serve, and improved academic outcomes for them.

The total cost of this pilot project for one year is $50,000, and we have already received commitments for half of this amount from other funders. Your investment of $25,000 would complete the funding we need to fully implement this pilot. We are very excited by the prospect of partnering with your foundation and appreciate your consideration of our request.

3. Organizational background

The organizational background section of a grant proposal is sometimes referred to as the applicant description. Regardless of what it's called, this is the part where you explain what your nonprofit is all about. This is the space to brag a little bit, but do not overcook it. This section should not run over three pages. Only include information that will help establish your organization's credibility and convince a funder that you are capable of executing your proposed project or program. Make a strong case for why you can be trusted as a responsible steward of grant funds. Your aim here is to convince them that your nonprofit is financially stable, well-managed, has a clear mission, understands community needs, has a strong board and great team, is popular and respected, and does fantastic, much-needed work.

Describe your nonprofit including when and how it originally came to be. Who founded it? Why did they start it, and who is served by it? Share your mission statement and outline how all activities cascade from it. You can include a brief needs statement along with an overview of your programs. After explaining your organizational philosophy through the story of where it came from and its evolution to date, it's time to write more about the processes that underpin your activities. Include a detailed breakdown of previous major initiatives and particularly notable achievements that relate to the proposed project. A bulleted list usually works well for this purpose. Testimonials and statistics may be included sparingly to underscore a track record of success. Call out any awards or external recognition your nonprofit has received.

Be sure to include the full legal name of your nonprofit, its charitable status, physical locations, and a summary of the overall budget including past and current funding sources. Explain its position in the community and mention any collaboration partners. Make note of why your services do not overlap, highlighting the aspects of your nonprofit that make it unique.

Organizational history represents an important part of the proposal, giving a funder additional confidence that your nonprofit is qualified to undertake this work. After reading this section, they should come away with no doubt that this is the right organization to do the job and the belief that your team has the ability, experience, and resources to succeed. You may touch on the backgrounds of key leaders and those who will be directly involved with implementation with a brief statement about your staff, volunteers, and board, but avoid going into too much detail about organizational structure unless specifically requested. Focus on concisely summarizing your organization's history, current programs, and audience served.

4. Problem statement/needs assessment

The purpose of this section is to paint a compelling picture of a gap you have identified. If you research and present your problem statement well, this will go a long way toward supporting your request for funding. Keep this section brief— ideally one page or less— and avoid using jargon. Establish the need for your project or program. Outline the consequences of not funding the project and these needs going unmet. The trick here is striking the perfect balance. You need to communicate the necessity of your proposed project or program, without being pessimistic. Aim to convey a sense of optimism that your initiative will provide a solution to the need. In other words, it must be an urgent yet solvable problem.

The basic elements of a well-written needs statement include a general description of the situation that clearly and concisely defines the need. Clarity is essential. Remember that a well-defined problem is one that can be solved whereas a vague problem cannot. Provide as much context and history as you can so the funder can fully understand the issue at hand. Document the need, which should be well supported with evidence— as statistical facts, research, and expert views. Any data cited needs to be as recent as possible and traced back to reputable, unbiased, and authoritative sources.

Do not stop at simply describing the symptoms. Demonstrate your thorough understanding of the problem. Why is it a problem? Who else sees it as such? What will happen if it is not resolved? Identify the barriers to addressing the need. What is standing in the way of a resolution? What is currently being done? Once you have clearly established the status quo, paint a picture of what's possible. Describe the gap between what exists now and what ought to be instead. If your project goes ahead, what change will occur as a result? How will people be impacted? Be realistic about what can be accomplished within the lifespan and constraints of the grant.

Focus on the needs of the target population to be served, rather than your organization or its needs. If mentioned, these should be articulated within the context of the community. The hero of your story should always be the clients or community you serve. Help the funder understand the challenges this audience faces and how your nonprofit serves as their guide. In too many of our stories, we tend to portray ourselves as the hero. As you begin to craft your grant proposals, position your nonprofit as the sidekick. Help the reader understand the hero of the story and the challenges they face and how you will serve as their guide. Cast the need or problem as the antagonist. For example, if your target audience is children and the main issue facing them is economic struggle, you would frame poverty as the enemy and your social support programs as the solution. This will help galvanize a reader into taking action. Statistics are ultimately impersonal, but you can put a face to the problem by building in a case study. A real-life example of the problem and how it has impacted someone's life cannot be underestimated. Highlight an individual your nonprofit has served and who benefited from a positive result. Make it real by adding the element of human interest. Their transformation arc will be key to your proposal.

Sample problem/needs statement

Many youths enter adulthood facing a lifetime of poverty as a result of the environment they were raised in. Those who fail to finish high school are among those most at risk. "Their risk is greatest; their hardship is most profound; and their current and future costs to our communities are the most significant." (Moving youth from risk to opportunity - Kids Count, 2004, The Annie E. Casey Foundation)

Children from the poorest families generally miss out on exposure to books and other printed content, as well as the modeling of verbal skills—often relying on access to materials via public institutions, which provide unequal resources across communities. They have fewer books in their homes, fewer books available in their school and classroom libraries, and live further from public libraries compared to children from middle and upper-income families. This is compounded by the fact that some schools and teachers are simply not equipped to teach these students. (Poverty and Literacy Development: Challenges for Global Educators, 2011, Bernard J King.)

Illiteracy remains one of the modern world's greatest

shortcomings. Not only does it limit the full development of an individual's capacity and their participation in society, it hinders them in everyday activities like reading labels and signs to less frequent but high-stakes activities like deciphering contracts. According to the OECD, adults with higher levels of reading literacy are more likely to be employed and to earn higher incomes. This disparity will only widen as information and communication technology continues to develop and play a larger part in society. (England & Northern Ireland (UK) – Country Note –Survey of Adult Skills first results, 2013, OECD)

Our programs are designed to help at-risk students catch up to their peers, improve their literacy and numeracy skills, and encourage them to graduate from high school. As their academic performance improves, so too does their self-confidence—providing a foundation for future excellence and success. We aim to ultimately assist young people in transitioning into adulthood, completing their education, and progressing into further training or full-time employment. In improving their lot in life today, we are equipping them for a more promising future.

5. Project description/Program description

This section is about making a case for support. Now that you have established the problem, what do you intend to do about it? Introduce your project or program here. Explain how this solution advances your mission and how it ties back to the funder's mandate. Make it easy for them to see exactly how you plan to tackle the issue by demonstrating how you have developed a thoughtful strategy to effectively address that need. Include details of any steps you have already taken to remedy it.

Think of this part as your chance to make a broad case for your project or program and convince the grant giver to commit to financial support. A compelling project explanation includes a description of a community need and presents a plan to remedy it. When writing this section, ensure you answer the *who, what, when, where, why,* and *how* questions that relate to the project. Provide a summary of the work plan—what exactly is to be done—as well as plans to market and promote the project and plans to adequately resource it. A timeline of program activities can be incorporated into the project description. Consult the grant guidelines for preference, and if there is no separate component for plan timings, then weave it into this section.

6. Program goals and objectives

This section identifies expected outcomes and benefits in clear, measurable terms. It is intended to communicate that you fully understand the situation and have a realistic grasp of your impact. Describe the outcomes of your proposed work once funded and implemented, detailing the change you anticipate it will deliver for the community. This is where you have to convey that your vision is worthwhile and that your objectives are achievable. Goals and objectives should tie back to your need statement. Aim to keep this section to one or two pages.

A goal is a general statement encompassing the outcomes your program or project hopes to bring about. Goals are visionary, broad, abstract, and difficult to measure in any objective way. Common keywords you may want to use in your project or program goals include *deliver, develop, establish, produce, provide, improve,* and *increase.* Objectives represent a step towards achieving that goal and are precise, concrete, and measurable. Goals articulate a bird's eye picture of your vision, and objectives detail what that looks like at ground level. For example, a goal might be to improve literacy rates in your city. The objective might be to provide 1,000 children in the area with weekly support from a reading buddy or tutor in the next calendar year.

One strategy for structuring this particular section is to break it down into direct subsections of individual goals. Describe an overarching goal, then refine it into one or more narrower objectives with specifics. Think of each objective as being a tangible result of an action, rather than an action in its own right. Structuring it in this way will clearly signal to your funder that your nonprofit fully understands its goals and can link those to realistic, actionable plans. Remember to check that you are regularly referencing your statement of need in this section to ensure consistency and relevance between the two.

Provide quantifiable measures for each objective and specify the target audience. Objectives could be focused on process and describe a specific output or focused on impact by describing an outcome. Ideally, structure these using the SMART framework: specific, measurable, attainable, realistic, and time bound. This shows you have put serious thought into creating your objectives and have a firm grasp on what is achievable.

7. Methods and strategy

The methods and strategy section is your plan of attack, where you take the big idea outlined in the proposal and carry this through to the reality of how you will make it happen. Whereas the previous sections of your grant proposal have addressed the *who*, *what*, and *why* of your plan, this is where you will more fully explain the *how* of your proposed programming. It essentially serves as the heart of your application and therefore should be the longest section—usually spanning several pages. This calls for a full explanation with details about the exact steps you will take at each stage and how you will implement them. Funders are looking for a logical, robust plan that will lead to the outcomes you have described.

You might choose to format this section as a chronological description with tactics tied to a timeline or, alternatively, as sub-sections for each of your objectives. Outline whom the program will serve, how they will be selected, and why this method is a good fit for them. Has this approach worked before for your organization or for similar nonprofits in this space? Are you using best practice or modifying it to suit the specific needs of your audience? Is it efficient and cost-effective? Does it work well for the nature of the problem? Describe the ways in which you will achieve the objectives. Provide a fully fleshed out model with explanations and visuals wherever possible. How will you execute the project? What are the key activities? Be mindful of any potential problems and outline alternative strategies you might deploy in response. Explain which staff/volunteers will be involved at each step, when they come in, and the roles they will play. Be sure to describe any partnerships that you will draw on, too.

How are you preparing for the project? Are there enough people who are trained and ready to deliver? Is there board and community support? What other resources are required? Connect this to the time frame. How will you meet key milestones? Activities should be structured in a way that the project moves steadily toward the desired results.

Write this section imagining that the reader knows nothing about your nonprofit or project. Try to follow up any complex technical sentences with one that provides a shorter explanation. Continually relate actions back to the project's original goals and need statements throughout the section. In addition, mention how you plan to keep stakeholders and donors up to date along the way.

Sample methods and strategy

In order to achieve the objectives for our Latino Community Pilot Program, ABC Youth will employ the methods outlined below. Our confidence in these methods is backed by their previous use by fellow non-profit organizations in neighboring cities, where they have been tested and proven by Rising Stars and Active Alliance. We have consulted with representatives from both of those organizations, and their advice helped shape our plans for this pilot.

For a detailed timeline, please see the appendices to this proposal.

Sample objective

Increase the number of Latino-identifying students enrolled in our after-school program by 35% by the end of the calendar year.

Sample method

We have already set up a working group to support this pilot and will establish an outreach committee led by two of our Latino board members who are fluent in Spanish.

We will hire two additional tutors, recruit a volunteer driver/facilitator, and obtain a van to provide optional drop-off services for students who require transportation home.

We will develop a formal referral system with other community organizations and agencies.

Staff will track students' progress at the beginning and end of each term. A program assistant will formally track each person's learning progress.

8. Evaluation plan

Just as projects vary, so too will evaluation techniques. Your approach will be informed by the measures of success you have outlined in your objectives. Failing to spell out how you intend to measure results can mean the difference between a successful application and a rejection. A solid evaluation plan has the added benefit of providing a guiding document and schedule for your team to follow throughout the project. If you are struggling to hit those metrics, this will help you identify the problem areas and adjust accordingly.

When planning an evaluation, start by considering what questions need to be answered. How will your team measure progress? What will define success? Set out some concrete, quantifiable metrics. Be clear about the short-term and long-term benefits, what information will be recorded and tracked, and which research or assessment methods will be used. Keep in mind the difference between outputs such as "implementing a new system to be used by 10 staff" and outcomes, such as "eliminating double-handling, reducing time spent on data entry by three hours each week." One is delivery-focused, while one is focused on results and change. Outputs could refer to the number of people served or number of classes delivered, and these are important to know for the purposes of resource allocation. When it comes to outcomes, benefits can include changes in behaviors, skill levels, attitudes, values, or conditions. Funders share your nonprofit's interest in outcomes and impact. Outcome measures can demonstrate real value in return for their financial support. They can also help your organization to improve your programs, develop long-term plans and budgets, and provide strategic direction.

Decide whether you will use quantitative, qualitative, or a combination of methods. Quantitative data is about hard counts; qualitative information explores experiences and feelings. Each has a role to play in different types of evaluations, and you may need both types, depending on your project. Articulate the reason behind your choice and ensure the evaluation approach aligns with your objectives and methods. Describe who will collect and analyze information, at what points they will do so, and how. You may conduct an internal assessment with your staff or hire outside expertise to carry out the evaluation. Qualitative methods can include focus groups, questionnaires, or surveys. Quantitative data may be gleaned from sources like scores on pre and post-tests or records of program participants. Along with end goals, plan for periodic evaluation at key milestones during the project lifecycle. At the end of your project, an evaluation report should be able to conclude whether the project or program achieved its initial goals and objectives. It should also speak to any changes made along the way and why, along with any unexpected problems or benefits that arose.

Your entire grant application should bring the funder along on a journey from introducing a problem to be solved, through your proposed solution, to a positive outcome. Make sure you have outlined logical steps to take your project from beginning to end, showing them how their input makes all the difference and how you will track the impact.

Sample evaluation plan

We have a plan in place to measure the success of our after-school program. This is designed to evaluate what information the students have learned over the course of the semester. At the beginning of the term, program facilitators issue a preliminary test to gauge a baseline and follow up at the end of the term with a similar test. In addition, at the end of each session, participating teachers are encouraged to fill out a detailed questionnaire so we can continue to improve on an already outstanding program.

The program is also regularly assessed by external evaluators. This outside panel of professionals is working with program staff to create a more sophisticated process that is still practical to deliver and does not unduly burden the facilitators. The aim is to build a clearer picture of the program's long-term impact on participating youth.

9. Sustainability

Sustainability is about finding ways to meet your present needs and future needs, using resources wisely with a view to the long term. Before investing in your project or program, a potential funder—be it a foundation, corporation, or government agency—will want to know how you plan to support your project on an ongoing basis. They want to ensure this particular workstream has a future beyond the window of time their funding provides. No funder wants to think that their grant will only cover a project for a short time. They are looking for long-term impact, not a quick win. They also want to know that your nonprofit is financially healthy and has a sustainable long-term outlook. Convince the funder that there is a way to continue the work after the grant expires. Will it continue to need the same level of funding, or will costs diminish over time? Capital construction projects have obvious sustainability issues upfront. A funder will seek reassurance that you can operate and maintain the facility once it has been completed.

Think of the sustainability section of your grant as the sequel to the story you have been telling so far throughout your proposal. How will that story continue? Where will you take it from there? Provide a roadmap that shows a clear plan for fundraising to continue operating and serving your community. Funders will be interested in both the short-term and long-term benefits outlined in your application.

Exactly how a project might be continued depends on its specific nature and design. Programs can be scaled by leveraging volunteers alongside staff as well as through partnerships and collaborations. Charging for services may be an option; this could be a flat fee or charged on a sliding scale based on individual income. Annual fundraisers are a common way to engage donors, as are membership and major-gifts programs. Naturally, ensure you are optimizing online channels and cause marketing to their full potential for giving. Corporate sponsorships—partnering with businesses on galas or charity runs—or employer-based fundraising campaigns are another avenue to explore. You could also consider potential entrepreneurial approaches that might generate additional revenue through selling products such as greeting cards or consumables and ventures like coffee stands, markets, or second-hand stores. Finally, account for other expected grant income going forward and ensure you are applying for all government funding— local, regional, and national— that your nonprofit qualifies for.

Any of these methods, along with any others you may think of, can act as effective strategies to continue to cover your nonprofit's activities. In your grant application, describe in detail which exact strategies you envision using. Include any information about hiring additional staff or contractors if that is indeed part of your ongoing execution plan.

At this point, if a funder has read this far into your proposal, they may have developed a genuine interest in your clients and the service you propose to offer. Now that they are invested in your story and vision, do not leave them hanging. Give them the confidence they need to trust that this project or program will go on and that your charity can remain healthy for years to come in order to deliver it.

Sample sustainability section

Over the past 12 months, ABC Youth has approached several new foundations for support. We are now delighted to report that we have received grants from the Northern Foundation (for technical assistance and capacity building), the Children's Foundation (for program delivery), and the Regional Community Foundation (for operating expenses).

Thanks to support from the Northern Foundation, we were able to hire an experienced fundraising consultant who is now working with our board of directors. Her mandate is to develop and implement a strategic fundraising plan, including an expanded annual giving program. Growing a larger base of individual donors will help to secure our financial future and diversify our income sources. This will complement our grant-funded streams; we currently have three active pending proposals, requesting a total of $75,000.

10. Budget

The budget identifies the costs to be met as part of your proposed project or program and the methods used to work out those costs. This will go a long way toward assuring a funder that your proposed activities are realistic and sustainable. In addition, a well-organized and formatted budget will make it much easier for them to digest and judge the financial viability of your application in order to make a decision. Ensure you have a good grasp of all the requirements of a specific grant before creating a detailed budget. Some will ask for more information, such as detailed overhead expenses, than others. Many grant givers also provide budget templates that must be submitted with the proposal. If this is the case, adapt your budget to fit within the provided form. Otherwise, the key thing to bear in mind when tackling this crucial section of a grant proposal is to be both thorough and realistic.

The funder needs to know exactly how much money you are requesting and where specifically you plan to direct it. This is especially important when you are approaching multiple funders. They may well be concerned about potentially funding something that is already being supported by someone else. Include any other expected sources of income; for example, you should disclose funds contributed by other parties. It can be helpful to include a brief overview of your regular funding sources as well. Your budget should reflect an appropriate level of anticipated funding from this particular grant giver. Do not give them a reason to second-guess your request. If what you are asking for is wildly out of line with the amounts they typically grant, you will appear out of touch. Likewise, if it doesn't line up with the scale of your project, it is bound to raise questions about how well you understand the reality of the situation. You will have a fiduciary duty to the grantor, so you need to ensure what you are asking for is within the realm of what you can achieve. Not only will this improve your chances of winning a grant, but it also means you are not setting up unrealistic expectations. Remember that you will have to deliver on whatever you promise once those funds are received.

Ideally, you would have a good idea of the funding organization's position and guidelines along with your initial project estimates, making this a fairly straightforward exercise. Document everything in detail; you need to clearly justify the level of funding needed to support your project. A seasoned program officer can easily spot padding in a budget, as well as when an application has underestimated costs. When finalizing your budget, go through your methods and strategies again taking note of every area that will require expenditure of resources. Include descriptions and hard numbers for each one. These could include staff and travel costs, fringe benefits, equipment, or indirect overheads.

OTHER SUPPORTING ELEMENTS

This section is for content that you would like to get in front of a funder but may not fit the main proposal. These attachments help them to get a clearer picture of your nonprofit or your proposed work. They can also serve as proof to back up statements you have made. Examples could include letters of support, resumes of key personnel, proof of charity status, clippings of media coverage, testimonials, etc. Do not go overboard; think quality rather than quantity.

Letters of support can provide further backing for the case you are making in your grant application. These are testimonials that speak to your nonprofit's track record of success and ability to deliver, illustrating that other individuals, businesses, and organizations believe you can get the job done. They show that others outside your nonprofit believe in the merit of your proposal. Each letter of support adds to the already compelling picture you are painting in your grant application providing further persuasive reasons why a funder should get on board. Although a letter of support will not necessarily seal the deal, it can certainly make your grant proposal more competitive.

A letter of support could come from a key stakeholder, a significant donor, a partner organization, a political representative, a community leader, or someone who would benefit from the service you would be providing. The stronger the reputation of the individual or organization providing the testimonial, the more weight their letter of support will carry. An ideal letter of support would not only communicate enthusiasm about your nonprofit's work and lend credibility to your application but include some sort of commitment of resources. The exact nature of that support would obviously depend on the circumstances. A local business might offer a gift in kind. A donor might pledge a specific amount of money. A corporation might commit to giving staff some pro bono hours to spend on volunteering to help your nonprofit. The more evidence you can offer that the funder will not be alone in supporting your project or program, the better. This improves the likelihood that your proposal will be well received.

You may wish to include specific details about board members and staff. While this might feel odd, if there is significant relevant expertise to highlight here, then including biographies or even resumes for key personnel is completely appropriate. If you do not, nobody else is going to talk up your people. Teams are critical to execution; remember that your team's connection to the problem and deep understanding of it uniquely qualifies you to solve it. Consider what skills are most important for achieving the task at hand and draw a clear connection that establishes how each person will help accomplish it. What key competencies make them so impressive? What similar successes have they previously had? Paint a picture of a cohesive team coming together to deliver an essential project to benefit their community.

Finally, quality testimonials can potentially change the entire context of your grant proposal. There's nothing more compelling than feedback from the people your organization serves. A good testimonial tells a story of transformation. What was the person's original starting point, where did they end up, and how specifically did your project or program help? You may tidy up basic spelling and punctuation corrections but let your subject's authentic voice shine through without being filtered or polished. Telling your story through a human lens brings a diversity of voices that helps your proposal stand out even after the numbers have been forgotten.

Testimonials can be found all around you in the thank you notes your nonprofit receives, in emails, and in impromptu conversations. You can also recruit strong testimonials by asking specific questions in follow-up surveys, such as: What aspects of the program were most valuable for you, and why? If you do not get the types of responses you are looking for, do not hesitate to follow up and dig a little deeper. Testimonials are a powerful way to illustrate why your donors keep coming back and why your team is so committed to your mission.

MORE TEMPLATES AND SAMPLES TO GET YOU STARTED

Now that you have a clear picture of what goes into a proposal and how to approach the various sections of a grant application, here are some templates and samples to give you inspiration. Always give yourself plenty of time to work on each application. According to research from GrantStation (2019), developing a strategic plan and writing the grant application took up to five days each for 60% or more of respondents surveyed. Starting early and working on one component at a time will make the process smoother and result in a more compelling proposal overall.

Here is a general structure you can follow to format your grant application.

1. Proposal template

GRANT NAME: ✎___

DATE SUBMITTED: ✎___

SUBMITTED TO: ✎___

SUBMITTED BY: ✎___

I. PROJECT DESCRIPTION (problem statement, goals and objectives, target population, project activities, key staff)

✎___

II. SUCCESS CRITERIA (measurable outcomes)

✎___

III. ORGANIZATIONAL BACKGROUND

✎___

IV. CURRENT PROGRAMS, ACTIVITIES, AND ACCOMPLISHMENTS

✎___

V. GOALS & OBJECTIVES

✎___

VI. TIMELINE

✎___

VII. BUDGET

BUDGET PERIOD START AND END DATES

✎___

Income		Expenses	
Source	Amount	Use	Amount
Total		Total	
Net income			

LONG-TERM SOURCES / STRATEGIES FOR FUNDING

✎___

VIII. EVALUATION

✎___

2. Sample LOI

Jane Smith

Program Officer

Blue Sky Community Foundation

123 Hill Rd

Central City

Dear Ms. Smith:

Thank you for reading this letter of inquiry to your Blue Sky Community Foundation. We hope to ascertain your interest in receiving a full proposal for our Central City ABC Youth Latino Community Pilot Program. We respectfully request your consideration for a grant of $25,000.

This project represents an expansion of our current services and marks our first dedicated outreach effort to the burgeoning local Latino population. We plan to engage with them to drive uptake of our after-school programs, activities, and other related services.

Our pilot program lands squarely within your foundation's key areas of interest—at the intersection of investing in underprivileged young people to help them realize their full potential and providing essential community services and information to minority groups.

Our facility serves as a community hub for local youth and their families. Established in 2012, it now serves more than 60 young people each day. Our mission is to support them in achieving their best in academics, sports, and the arts.

Our latest surveys point to an extremely high satisfaction rate among youth and their parents of 97 percent. We provide nutritious snacks, educational tutoring, creative outlets, social opportunities, and physical exercise throughout the year.

The population of the neighborhoods we serve is expected to increase by 22 percent over the next two decades. Approximately 63 percent of them are projected to identify as Latino. Many of these families are at or below poverty level and have limited individual access to reliable transport. To help boost uptake of our after-school programs, we plan to begin offering optional transfer services, dropping off students at home after classes finish.

Our one-year pilot program objectives include:

1. increasing the number of Latino students enrolled by 35%

2. recruiting 10 more volunteers to facilitate our after-school program
3. improving test scores among participating youth as measured at pre-set intervals throughout the year

The total cost of our pilot program for one year is $50,000. Half of that has already been accounted for thanks to commitments from both the county government and other funders.

Your investment of $25,000 would cover the remainder of the funding needed to fully implement the pilot project. Our board of directors is eager to embark on this project, and we have received expressions of interest from volunteers.

We appreciate your consideration of this exciting project and look forward to hearing from you soon.

Sincerely,

Sarah Green

Executive Director

ABC Youth

3. Sample grant proposal

Cover letter

Alex Hill

Program Officer

Northern Foundation

123 Whitehall Rd

Central City

Dear Mr. Hill:

The JOY (Just Older Youth) Association is seeking a grant to provide support services to seniors in Eastern City. The elderly (65+) comprises 25% of the population in this area. Retirees often struggle to adjust to life after work and declining health. Our work spans two complementary streams: organizing social outings and events for retirees and delivering meals to the homes of seniors with mobility restrictions.

Funding in the amount of $130,250 is requested to support the meal delivery program. The total cost of the meal delivery service for one year is $180,000, the rest of which will be covered by contributions from local businesses. Your investment would cover the outstanding balance required to deliver this project.

Our work aligns closely with your foundation's key priority: supporting and advocating for our senior citizens. Since our organization's inception, we have continued to expand our services engaging with an average of 4 percent more local seniors each year. We currently deliver regular meals to 170 local households. The recipients are seniors aged between 67 and 90 on fixed incomes with little or no family support.

The population of the neighborhoods we serve is projected to grow by 10 percent over the next decade. Due to the aging population at large and the amenities in this area, 72 percent of new arrivals are likely to be aged 65 or older. Many of these senior citizens live on their own.

Our objective for the next calendar year is to deliver meals to an additional 10 percent of local seniors, who can opt to receive deliveries on a daily, twice weekly, or weekly basis.

Thank you for your consideration of our proposal. We look forward to hearing from you soon.

Sincerely,

Alana White

Executive Director

Joy Association

Executive summary

The JOY Association in Eastern City is seeking a grant to expand our meal delivery program with the objective of ensuring all local seniors have adequate, nutritious food to eat while fostering a sense of community connection in the process. We intend to deliver meals to an additional 17-20 households in the calendar year ahead. Funding in the amount of $130,250 is requested to support this program.

Organization

The JOY Association was established in 2017 by a group of five seniors aged between 60 and 85. These empty nesters were neighbors who found themselves at a loss after major life transitions such as stopping work, becoming widowed, or having their families move away for jobs. Spearheaded by May Burke, they sought to organize activities and support services catering to the specific needs of seniors. We now serve 250 older adults each week with a variety of programs and services, including delivering regular meals to the homes of 170 seniors. Our mission is to help older people maintain a healthy, independent lifestyle and maintain their quality of life.

Our purpose is as follows:

1. facilitate social interaction and community involvement
2. foster independence and dignity
3. break down common myths and stereotypes about aging
4. encourage living life to the fullest

Our program director, Jennifer Reeves, has an extensive background in public service. She previously held a number of policy roles focused on retirement and the aging population. She is frequently quoted in the media as an expert in this area, most recently on Channel Five's morning show *Breakfast* and in *M2 Woman* magazine. Our coordinator, Shaun Freeman, began with us as a volunteer five years ago and has served in various capacities across our two main programs in that time. He was named a Local Hero in last year's National Volunteer award scheme.

Needs statement

Many older people in Eastern City struggle with the ever-increasing costs of living, including the costs of buying groceries. One in three recipients says their delivered meal is the main source of food for that day.

In addition, social isolation is a major issue. Most of our recipients feel disconnected from the fabric of society. They yearn for social interaction. They relish their independence and do not want to feel like a burden on their families but do not wish to enter assisted living. Many seniors can easily go for days without seeing other people. It is not uncommon for an older person who lives alone to fall, injure themselves, and be unable to call for help.

Overall, social isolation is associated with poor health, increased risk of dementia, and premature death. Our service can act as a lifeline in this regard.

Program description

We deliver fresh meals to recipients' homes either daily, twice a week, or once a week. Typical meals meet nutritional guidelines and can be tailored to suit dietary needs or preferences. Nine out of 10 recipients say this service helps them to live independently.

Our meal delivery service helps many elderly and disabled people maintain their independence and provides much needed regular social contact. Over half of recipients say their interaction with the person delivering their meal is the only social contact they have that day. Our delivery drivers often stop to chat, essentially conducting informal check-ins, which is especially important for recipients with more complex health issues.

They can help recipients address safety hazards in the home or assist them with any other essential tasks they may be struggling with on their own, such as changing light bulbs or managing laundry. The service has the potential to reduce the caring burden, giving peace of mind to family members who do not live close by and cannot regularly visit their loved ones.

Often recipients also form relationships with other meal recipients and wider Joy Association regular members.

"Since I've stopped working and my children moved to the other side of town, I've felt increasingly lonely without anything to fill my days. It's hard to get motivated to cook for one person. It's so nice to see a friendly face on my doorstep with a hot meal in hand to boot." - June, meal recipient

June's husband died many years ago and her remaining siblings live overseas or out of town. Her two sons recently moved away to be closer to their jobs and their own children's schools. She downsized to a smaller property in a nearby community and found herself without much of a support network. She developed a bond with the local volunteer who delivered her meals (initially weekly, now daily) and now regularly attends our social outings with other JOY members to croquet, arthouse films, botanic gardens, etc.

Goals and objectives

Our goal is to empower local seniors to live life to the fullest. This program supports older people to live independently in their own homes and age in place. The main objective of our meal delivery service is expanding our current base of recipients and maintaining or improving our 95% rating on satisfaction surveys.

Program budget

Supplies (mainly ingredients, including $23,890 in donations from local manufacturers and retailers) - $155,000

Packaging and other supplies/equipment - $9,000

Fuel costs - $5,000

Staff costs (including three volunteer delivery drivers) - $11,000

Total costs = $180,000

Overall, our organization is funded through private/foundation grants (51%), government grants (34%), corporate sponsorships (10%), and donations/fundraising (5%). We have twice received funding through the central government's Age Concern Fund for our programs.

In the future, we plan to explore options to increase the sustainability of our operations, such as more recyclable or compostable packing, strategic use of frozen ingredients for variety and convenience, or hosting shared meals at a community center to facilitate social inclusion. We already provide transfers for seniors on our social outings and could extend this service to encompass transport to shared meals.

We also intend to intensify our fundraising efforts and cultivate more individual donors. Additionally, one of our corporate supporters, Acme International, has expressed interest in sponsoring one of our delivery routes. Flamegrill, a restaurant situated next to the local Coles supermarket that provides us with many fresh and dry ingredients, has also offered the use of its facilities for cooking purposes once a week.

Evaluation

We track the number of meals delivered every week. This will be updated and reported each quarter to monitor growth. In addition, recipients are surveyed every six months to assess their satisfaction with the service. This is centrally managed by our coordinator. Delivery drivers dispense and collect the surveys when they visit each recipient at home. These are then analyzed by the coordinator and disseminated more widely.

STRATEGICALLY POSITIONING AND PITCHING YOUR NONPROFIT

Finally, it bears repeating that regardless of how worthy your project or program is, how you *position* your nonprofit has everything to do with your odds of success. If there's one thing I want you to take away from this, it's the importance of retaining a strategic mindset and pitching well.

Alignment matters. If you have the choice, pitch to an organization that is a natural fit and that will be excited about your project from the get-go. Building on a warm connection will only further increase your chances of success. Your proposal should clearly demonstrate how what you are doing fits in with the areas they already know well and prioritize. Speak their language and play up common interests. Remember that you have limited space to make your charitable cause memorable. The reality of the human attention span and memory is that both are limited. Trying to pack too much in and convey everything only results in the reader retaining nothing at all. If they come away only remembering one thing from your proposal, what should that be?

Foundations and nonprofits share a common goal— improving outcomes in the areas in which they operate. Although it can be difficult to quantify these goals, it's imperative to focus on performance measures and find a way to present your desired impact in a clear, measurable manner to funders. After all, many projects begin with great promise only to wind up with dashed hopes, limited impact, and uncertain prospects for the future. Remember that although you are asking for money, it doesn't mean they are above you. Consider yourselves as equals engaging in a dialog over a potential deal. Go in with the confidence to have a transparent conversation. Be honest about what stage you are at, what you have accomplished so far, and what you envision for the future. Your vision for the end game should be magnetic and infectious. Convey exactly why you are so driven to solve this problem and why you and your team are the ones to solve it.

As publicly traded organizations are increasingly held to account for their risks, nonprofits can benefit from applying a similar lens to their work and addressing this upfront in proposals. A few institutions are also beginning to look for this component in applications. They are naturally receptive to the role of risk management; it's in their best interests to ensure grant recipients are spending with a conservative approach. It's difficult to truly understand your priorities without a clear understanding of the risks faced across all areas, from governance and compliance to development, finances, operations, and reputation management.

When putting a grant proposal together, consider organizational risk—in relation to funding, governance, and people—as well as strategic risk and executional risk.

To get a picture of the potential risks associated with your project, have everyone involved come together to conduct an initial risk inventory. Brainstorm all the possible risks that could pop up throughout its lifecycle. Rate the likelihood of each risk occurring, and quantify the impact it would have on time, cost, and quality. Then, you can devise mitigation strategies accordingly, so you can be honest about the risks and how you will deal with them in your proposal. Instead of worrying about exposing organizational weaknesses, show that you are aware of weak spots and articulate how you will strategically deploy to get the job done for maximum efficiency and effectiveness. An experienced program officer is always looking for red flags. The fact is, they must reject the majority of applications they receive. Do not give them an easy reason to turn yours down.

CHAPTER ACTIVITY: CREATE YOUR PROPOSAL TEMPLATE

Of all the activities in this chapter, this will prove to be the most demanding and time consuming but doing it well will be the most rewarding. Set aside some time and go to a place where you are undisturbed with a piece of paper or your laptop. In two hours or less, you want to create a detailed document with the following:

- **Your organizational background** – What is your nonprofit about? How did it come to exist? Where are you registered (give legal name and physical address)? How long have you been operational? What are some of your achievements? What is your philosophy? What typical programs do you run? Who benefits from your work? Who do you partner with?

- **The problem you are solving** – What gap have you seen? Why is your project/program needed? What evidence is there that the problem is real (research, anecdotal evidence, etc.)?

- **How do you plan to solve it** – What solutions do you have for the problem? Who is the target population for your solution?

- **A project description with goals and objectives** – Why exactly are you asking for money? Is it a new project or an existing one? How would it/does it work? Who is in charge? Who would benefit from it? What are your goals and objectives? Make sure your goals are S.M.A.R.T.

- **Your operational strategy** – How will you make your goals a reality? Give a logical and robust plan for achieving the goals for your project. What are the key activities?
- **How you will assess success** – How will you measure results? What will success look like?
- **A timeline and a budget** – How long do you think the project will last? How will you spend the money, if you receive it, and how much are you asking for?

It should take you about 15 minutes to work on each bullet point. The bullet points represent some major sections in a grant proposal. Paint with broad strokes at this point. Include as much detail as you can and try to have fun while doing so. It will help your cause to do this exercise at the time of the day when you are most productive. If you are stuck, use the questions provided as prompts and detail your answers. After answering these questions, you will have proposal template answers that are specific to your nonprofit and your project that you can always tweak to suit the funding opportunity you are applying for.

6

GETTING YOUR NONPROFIT TO STAND OUT FROM THE REST

The grant landscape is becoming increasingly competitive. You should always be thinking about the best way to get your proposals to stand out from the crowd in order to win funding. It's easy to get tunnel vision when you've been immersed in your cause for a long time. In this chapter, I will offer ten strategic tips for planning and writing a grant application that stands out. Knowing who you are and what you stand for will be key to successfully selling your story.

TIPS TO HELP YOUR NONPROFIT STAND OUT

1. Prep your toolkit

Be prepared. Compile all your collateral in one place so that it's ready for you to pull out when needed. Many grants are only open for a short window of time. Having this material handy will make it much easier to write out a fantastic grant application when you get the opportunity. You can then spend your time crafting the most effective proposal possible without worrying about digging up supporting content. It also pays to have a similar arsenal of potential projects that you can draw upon. If a funding opportunity arises, you can match one of these concepts to the grant. You want to avoid getting into the situation where you are scrambling to shape a project to fit the criteria for a grant as opposed to serving the needs of your community.

2. Keep your funder in mind as you write

The people who read, assess, and score your proposals are human too. Whether they are paid staff or volunteers, it is important to write your application with your reviewer in mind. Make it as easy as possible for them to understand. Assume that the reader has never heard of your nonprofit and knows nothing about the community you serve, the problem you are solving, what you do, or how you do it. This application is all they have to go on, so you need to spell out everything they need to know. Since they do not inhabit your world, reduce or cut out industry-specific terminology. Explain acronyms the first time they are mentioned and use plain language wherever possible.

3. Follow the instructions/templates

Most of the time, there will be an application form to complete and guidelines you are expected to follow. There may be specific questions you need to answer and attachments you need to include. Follow any instructions to the letter. Respond to questions in the order in which they are listed and echo the terminology they use. After all, if you cannot take directions at this stage, the logical assumption would be that you probably will not follow directions when it comes to delivering reports or other follow-up items after you are awarded a grant.

4. Leave enough time

As previously mentioned, you may not get much time to write a proposal. Build in enough time for input or edits from other stakeholders. Do not miss this step, as outside feedback can help you make a stronger case. Make a list of all documents that need to be submitted, key dates for completing and reviewing drafts, and any other tasks involved—along with who is responsible for each.

5. Focus on strengths

Any charity can rattle off a mile-long laundry list of what they need: a new building, another staff member, or more equipment. Unfortunately, these are not compelling arguments for a funder who is looking to support change. A grant giver wants to know about your solutions to community challenges and the impact of your work. Present your proposal as coming not from a needy nonprofit at risk of going under but a healthy, viable, and competitive organization worthy of investment. Think along the lines of crafting a pitch not a request. Focus on presenting your strengths well and how these strengths can help you achieve your project outcomes. Narrow it down to the most relevant and important points. You might have ten great reasons, but taken as a whole, this might diminish their impact. Boiling it down to three sharp, succinct points that convey your strengths, however, can make for a more powerful case.

6. Ensure you are involving the right stakeholders

As you design your project, be sure to involve the right people. A stakeholder group that is critical to creating impactful programs is the population you serve. However, they are often overlooked in the process. Their input can show you exactly what they are struggling with, why they are struggling with it, and what can be done to break the cycle. This will strengthen the story you have to tell through your applications. If you can point to ways that your target audience helped to co-design your initiatives, this will lend extra credibility to your proposal in the eyes of a funder.

7. Include partners where relevant

Many non-profit organizations collaborate with other groups or agencies to deliver their services. Funders want to see that you are teaming up with other partners to address the root cause of the problems you are tackling. Quality partnerships add credibility to your proposal rather than detract from it. Collaborations can maximize the use of grant funds through coordinating services to the target population in the most efficient way. Outline how you will share resources and what each partner brings to the table. What role will they play? Define their involvement and how much they will do. Specify the type of contributions involved whether it's personnel, facilities, expertise, equipment, or cash.

8. Present a comprehensive budget

A budget is not just a matrix of numbers. Your budget narrative should clearly show to the reader how you plan to leverage other funds to deliver your project and what cost-saving measures you will deploy. Demonstrate that you have thought about how you intend to capitalize on all available resources to make the most out of a funder's investment. In relation to partnerships, be sure to detail any cash contributions that will come into play, as well as non-monetary contributions —also known as *in-kind* contributions.

9. Study other successful grant applications

There is no better way to improve than to learn from those who have gone before you. Reading successful grant proposals will help you hone your own grant writing skills. There are some samples provided in the previous chapter and many more available online at websites like candid.org and thegrantadvantage.net. Do not copy them blindly but read through them and take note of what works. Find ways to apply these principles in your own grant applications. Find ways to tell your own story and refine your own voice.

10. Do not give up

Writing winning grants is a unique skill that can be developed. If you are willing to dedicate the time and effort to learning, you will get out as much as you put in. While your first few attempts may not bear fruit, reach out to the funder and ask for feedback about what might have made your application stronger. Use that information to enhance subsequent proposals.

CROSS CHECK EVERYTHING AGAINST YOUR MISSION STATEMENT

You are guaranteed to stand out if your proposal remains true to everything you stand for as a nonprofit. By virtue of where you are located, what you do, and how you do it, your nonprofit is already unique. If you align everything to your mission statement, it will increase your chances to get the funding significantly. A mission statement is an important part of any organization's identity. It captures a vision, purpose, and target audience and can convey a lot to a potential grant giver. Use the mission statement you clarified in Chapter 1 to guide you to position your nonprofit in a compelling way in your proposals.

In a well written mission statement, there is a balance stricken between its role in your organization's public image and its role in internal communications and strategy. The mission statement guides you and your staff in all that you do. It also makes outsiders want to learn more about your organization and get involved, thereby helping attract funding. A great mission statement rallies everyone involved around a common goal, adding clarity to your operations. Think of it as a compass or your North Star in terms of evaluating options and making decisions. It's impossible to prioritize everything, so your mission statement can help you focus on the right things. Mission statements will help your entire nonprofit act consistently as well as influence your organizational culture. Your staff and volunteers want to believe in the work they do.

Make sure that your mission statement distills the essence of your organization into one or two sentences. It should explain why your nonprofit exists, whom it serves, and how. You can edit it if you find it to be inaccurate. It needs to be unambiguous and memorable.

Keep it concise, avoiding long or complex words or phrases, buzzwords, jargon, or generalities. Get specific, evoke emotions, and make it something that is easy to remember and repeat. To hone in on the value-add of your solutions, encourage participation from your working group. Collect insights and feedback from everyone you can: staff, board members, volunteers, partners, and supporters.

Powerfully written mission statements can help nonprofits stand out from the rest of the crowd. Take this one from Watts of Love: *Our mission is to bring people the power to raise themselves out of the darkness of poverty through solar lighting.* (Our Values - Watts of Love, 2021, Watts of Love). It inspires, communicates the organization's purpose, and clearly mentions the solution it offers. Alternatively, consider charity: water's mission statement: *charity: water is a non-profit organization bringing clean and safe drinking water to people in developing nations.* (About Us | charity: water, 2022, charity: water). It cuts to the chase touching on who the organization serves, where those people live, and what the organization actually does. In just a few words, it summarizes its purpose using terms anyone would understand. Finally, let's look at an example from First Descents: *First Descents provides life-changing, outdoor adventures for young adults impacted by cancer and other serious health conditions.* (Who We Are - First Descents, 2022, First Descents). In clearly specifying the age range served, this snappy mission statement is laser focused. The nonprofit's work is summed up with a compelling descriptor and packs a punch.

USE YOUR MISSION STATEMENT TO ENSURE ALIGNMENT

It is already clear so far that successfully winning grants rests on finding the right fit with similarly aligned grant givers. Clarity of purpose will help you sharpen your focus and narrow in on the most likely partners. Here are a few further tips for advancing your interests by prioritizing fit and building credibility to support your story. Double-check that your mission, objectives, and values truly align with the funder's. Something might seem like a good fit, but that does not mean it actually is. Closer inspection may yield some criteria that disqualify your nonprofit or reveal clashing values.

Compare the application deadline with the payout date. If the timelines do not match up with your project deadlines, then it simply is not the right grant to pursue at this time. Then, make sure that the funding available matches your project needs. If limits are not specified, do some further research; announcements of previous recipients can help you get a rough sense of the amounts typically awarded. How does that stack up against your projected costs? If you need $80,000 for a project, but the grantor has previously paid out an average of $3,000 per organization, it may not be the best fit. A grantmaker wants assurance that their funds will help you deliver your project, so you would need to explain where the rest of the funding would come from, outlining how this grant fits into your larger project funding strategy.

THE BOTTOM LINE: SELLING YOUR NONPROFIT'S STORY

Every charity has a story to tell about its organization and the impact of its work. As a grant writer, you need to believe in that story. If you have bought into it, you will be able to pitch it much more powerfully. While it is important to adhere to the rules when putting a proposal together, it is also essential to make sure your nonprofit's story comes across as well. Letting that unique voice and personality shine through will be crucial to convincing grantmakers to get on board. As a non-profit organization, your future hinges on your ability to secure outside funding, and the key to successful fundraising often lies in compelling story-telling.

All great stories have a setting, plot, strong characters, and satisfactory conclusion. Determine the main take-away of the story you want to tell beforehand. Then, begin with the who, where, and when of your nonprofit's origin story. Describe the setting; this is especially important when funders target a specific location. Lay out the problem or need and who it affects. Then, once you have established the obstacles, outline the desired outcome and the actions taken to reach the resolution.

When writing a grant, your natural inclination is usually to portray your nonprofit as the hero in your narrative. However, the real heroes are the people or population you serve. When crafting your project or program descriptions, instead think of your organization as their wise guide. Paint a picture of the problem or need faced by the hero and how, with your help, you can conquer that nemesis together. We instinctively connect with stories and become invested in seeing how a story arc plays out. The more captivating your narrative, the more likely you are to invigorate a reader into taking decisive action to support your cause. Take that problem and spin it into a narrative with a happy ending all around. You can try building a story around one of the individuals your project or program is help-ing. Describe their background, what their struggles are, and then how they will benefit specifically from the project. This will help make your grant proposal seem more real and impactful. Now, although they are not reflected directly in the story you have told so far, the funder will be a key character going forward. Consider their motivations and goals. Remind them that the story relies on them playing their part and make it clear how their contribution is going to make all the difference.

Inject passion into every facet of your proposal. Write with zest about your charity's founders and their driving purpose. Write with compassion about the problem you plan to solve using the grant funds. How can you bring to life the reality of what people are facing and the challenges they are juggling? Employ adjectives to convey the severity of the situation and use your needs statement to create tension. Likewise, use emotive language to illustrate the transformation and result.

When incorporating facts and figures, try to make use of tables and graphics, and contrast these with real-life scenarios. A case study showing how someone turned their life around as a result of your program is incredibly powerful. As the saying goes, a single death is a tragedy; a million deaths is a statistic. You do not need to try to cover every type of client you serve—just one or two relevant personas. If your nonprofit is young and your projects unproven, focus on your own staff and volunteers. Perhaps they have overcome their own hurdles and hardships and are now channeling that energy and focus for a greater good. You could also highlight how a key donor originally connected with your cause and has supported it ever since. Given word count restrictions, you may wonder how you are expected to fit all this into your application. Stories do not need to be lengthy. Even a few lines will suffice. Extract the juiciest, most colorful quotes and anecdotes that will land with the most impact.

When you boil it down, grant writing is a form of storytelling. Your story should convey the facts in a compelling manner, delivering an ultimately triumphant narrative that pays off for the reader and satisfies their need for a neat conclusion. Grant reviewers read a lot of proposals, so they gravitate towards those that are interesting and easy to read, as well as those that fit into the framework of what they are expecting to see. It is up to you to capture their attention, highlight how your work matches their priorities, and why that compatibility makes for a natural partnership.

CHAPTER ACTIVITY: PUT IT ALL TOGETHER AND CUSTOMIZE TO YOUR TOP PROSPECT

At this point, you have content for most sections of the proposal. The idea is to put them in the right format and to edit them to target the number one prospect you identified in Chapter four. Follow the format provided in the proposal sample in Chapter 5. Use the answers you have provided in Chapter 5 to fill out the relevant sections as follows:

- Your organizational background – organizational background
- The problem you are solving – needs/problem statement
- How you plan to solve it – program goals and objectives
- A project description with goals and objectives – project description
- Your operational strategy – methods and strategy
- How you will assess success – evaluation plan
- A timeline and a budget – budget and sustainability

Do not worry about sections like the cover letter and the executive summary that you do not have yet.

Simply fill out these sections and edit them to fit in with the prospect you will be sending the proposal to. Use the keywords they have used in their guidelines as much as is realistically possible. Highlight the places where your goals and missions align and make the proposal as compelling as you can. At this point, you can also create a story representing the typical person you help and add it to sections of your proposal, more so in the organizational background, problem you are solving, your strategy, and evaluation plan.

7

INSPIRATION FROM FUNDING INNOVATION

L ike venture capital firms, foundations and other grantmakers only fund a small percentage of the funding requests they receive. Venture capitalists typically have a significant impact on the start-ups they invest in, supporting the long-term growth of those companies. However, grant givers parcel out much smaller amounts to higher numbers of recipients over much shorter periods of time. Grants only cover a small portion of any nonprofit's expenses. That is why you need to get creative in your approach to fundraising.

It is time to start thinking beyond conventional grant giving. This chapter will delve into best practices and trends in the world of nonprofit funding. You will come away with fresh inspiration from innovation in philanthropic funding that you can apply to your own fundraising efforts. You will also find some additional resources to help with continuously sharpening up your grant writing at the end of this chapter.

GET INNOVATIVE IN YOUR OUTREACH

As a non-profit organization, much of your success hinges on connection with the community you serve and staying relevant. Prioritize getting active in your local area to build up brand recognition and to get to know the people who could well be your best supporters and advocates. Participate in local events like festivals and markets to get in front of potential donors and volunteers as well as people who may potentially benefit from your programs and services. A physical presence at a booth or stand provides a face for your nonprofit and will help raise awareness of your mission. If possible, try to mobilize a group of ambassadors to go out and engage with the public on a regular basis.

The work of a non-profit professional never ends. Building and cultivating relationships within your community will be an ongoing process. Consider hosting training events and seminars, which give your team an opportunity to practice their pitches and teach about what they know best. Sharing expertise will provide extra value to those who attend and help to promote your nonprofit in the process. These could even be held virtually. Think outside the box. Along with educational or professional development workshops and webinars, this could extend to art classes, performances, and shows. All of this helps to raise your organizational profile and cement what you are known for. The stronger your reputation, the stronger your grant applications will be.

ASK FOR MORE THAN MONEY

Cash is king, which is why fundraising usually takes up so much of a typical nonprofit's time and energy. But that is not to say it's the only thing your organization needs. Many nonprofits would benefit equally from non-monetary support such as hands-on help in molding strategies, prototyping new ideas, and building their systems and capability. Your grant applications can reflect the full scope of your needs if you know that the funding agency can help you potentially meet those.

In the venture capital world, funders often take a seat on the board of the companies they fund. This is less common in nonprofits, not least due to potential conflicts of interest and time constraints. That said, it is not entirely unheard of. According to Deloitte (2015), Draper Richards Kaplan Foundation, a global venture philanthropy firm, supports grantees' success by taking a seat on the board for three years. Precedent can also be seen in the case of New Profit—a funder of innovative nonprofits serving low-income Americans that operates much like a sophisticated venture capital firm. According to the Harvard Business Review (2010), New Profit performs rigorous analysis on potential recipients and actively manages its investments to increase their social impact. A partner serves on each nonprofit's board and becomes a day-to-day adviser helping the leadership team with everything from recruiting to refining its social change model. New Profit also helps the nonprofits in its portfolio develop measurement frameworks for impact and organizational performance and provides them with access to high-level strategic advisers. These advisers coach on strategy development and growth planning.

At a nonprofit where leaders are head-down working to create impact, core organizational functions are often underdeveloped. Funders can support organizations in building these skills, thus playing a more active role in their ultimate success. This could look like connecting a nonprofit to critical mentorship, training, and coaching opportunities. It could mean introducing them to other funders, influencers, media, and specialized professionals like accountants and lawyers. It could mean supporting outreach efforts, strategic planning, financial modeling, and communications strategy to shape public perceptions. Define whatever gaps you see in the skill sets of your team or strategy that currently weaken your nonprofit's resilience. Then you can hone in on how funders may be able to support you on remedying those, and which funders in particular may be best placed to help in that regard.

PRESENT HOW YOU ARE LEARNING AND IMPROVING

Implementing lasting change can often take years, if not decades. After taking a stake, investors typically engage with a start-up for as many as 10 years. Foundations work on a much shorter horizon. The typical timeframe of a grant leaves little time for recipients to come up with innovative programs or campaigns. However, you can play up the benefits of continuous learning and improvement for both funders and the wider system you operate within. Innovations often follow a long and winding path and accrue interesting smaller breakthroughs along the way that others in the field can leverage.

Social innovation is inherently risky. It is only through experimenting that new concepts can be tested and eventually proven. Trial and error yields constant learning. The nonprofit world could take a cue here from the world of entrepreneurship by embracing the principles of fast failure and radical transparency. Making our streams of successes and failures alike more public and creating a discourse around dissecting these lessons will benefit society as a whole. We can learn from what works and what does not only if failure is analyzed and shared widely. According to the European Venture Philanthropy Association (2015), this is why an increasing number of organizations are advocating for more openness in sharing stories of failures. The Canadian NGO Engineers Without Borders publishes an annual Failure Report (2017 Failure Report, 2017, Engineers Without Borders) in which engineers share their stories of failing and the lessons they learned as a result. This level of transparency—outlining what went wrong and why—benefits not just others in the organization, but those outside of it too.

Donors view nonprofits as the most likely organizations to develop solutions and instigate change but not always in isolation. A Fidelity (2016) study found that donors believe multiple groups have the best potential to find ways to overcome society's problems. They increasingly see both nonprofits and public-private partnerships as the most probable candidates to successfully address challenges. The idea of cross-sector collaboration, taking a broad view of stakeholders, is gaining traction. No single sector is charged with sole responsibility. It may be time to explore forming new partnerships with outside groups. For example, more and more universities are home to social change incubators, and businesses are increasingly building their social responsibility teams and capability. Nontraditional groups that are newer to the social sector have a particular opportunity to expand their reach and redefine their missions in the name of social impact.

To sustain organizational growth, you will need to look beyond the current round of funding. Consider proposing that a funder stays on board until your nonprofit is ready for the next stage of funding. According to the Harvard Business Review (1997), one organization that has successfully taken this approach is Cooperative Home Care Associates (CHCA). This New York-based, worker-owned cooperative provides health care to the elderly in their homes. When CHCA wanted to build on its success and expand its operations by launching a training institute, it approached a previous funder with a long-term plan for building self-sustaining cooperatives. That funder—the Charles Stewart Mott Foundation—then awarded CHCA a series of renewable grants over a seven-year period. Programs like this provide an incentive for funders to move away from the standard terms of just one or two years and toward longer-term periods where their grants can have more sustained impact. Meanwhile, another nonprofit, Family Service America, found success in pitching for funding for capacity building. Instead of proposing a new program, the organization laid out an analysis of its organizational needs. These ranged from recruiting and training to benchmarking and change management. Family Service America successfully convinced foundations to invest in strengthening its organizational capability as a way of driving program outcomes. (Virtuous Capital: What Foundations Can Learn from Venture Capitalists, 1997, Harvard Business Review).

GO BIG

Ask for too little in a grant application, and the funder may feel they could have more impact if they chose to fund a larger project instead. Think about the scale of your impact. Take a step back and look at the bigger picture while considering the context of the wider field you work within. When you see the whole landscape, what is missing? Which areas could you expand into? Finding powerful ideas with the potential to create lasting change requires you to do things differently from how you have always done them. It calls for exploring beyond the usual suspects to come up with new solutions. As you build a list of exciting opportunities, you should then prioritize these based on their potential for transformation. Try ranking each one according to the likely future impact it would have. Size matters when it comes to making a substantive impact on pervasive and complex societal problems. If there is one area where there's no excuse for thinking small, it's fundraising. Regardless of the size of your nonprofit, the cause you are fighting for is an important one. Make sure you give yourself appropriate credit for that.

Thinking big could mean launching an ambitious new program or campaign. It might mean going for new funding streams. It might even mean coming up with an innovative new growth strategy. As described in a Stanford Social Innovation Review (2007) article, nonprofits that achieve the most growth invest in talent and build structures that support a high-growth model. For instance, housing nonprofit Help USA created a team of more than 30 people to apply for and manage complicated government contracts. The Oregon Food Bank built a $10 million distribution center with the ability to handle both fresh and frozen food, dramatically expanding the range of donations it was able to accept (How non-profits get really big, 2007, Stanford Social Innovation Review). These are just a few examples of thinking differently and expanding your horizons.

FURTHER RESOURCES

If you want to learn from the pros, there is plenty of advice available out there. Institutions and universities alike provide grant writing advice that can be freely accessed online. For starters, some general resources can be found at The Writing Center website by the University of North Carolina. For more rigorous training, you may like to investigate courses or workshops, such as Effective Grant Proposal Writing from the University of Notre Dame. For further tips and tools from official sources, visit the US Government grants website or the Environmental Protection Agency web page on grants.

CHAPTER ACTIVITY: WRITE YOUR COVER LETTER AND EXECUTIVE SUMMARY

So far, you have a near complete proposal already customized to your top prospect. It is now time to write your executive summary and cover letter. If time has passed between your working on the previous chapter and now, go through all sections of your proposal before writing your executive summary. The executive summary is meant to provide a brief overview of everything included in your proposal. You are generally asking yourself this question: *What is the essential problem you are solving with this work?*

Be sure to frame the need or problem as a succinct query before shifting into providing the answer through your proposed project or program. What do you intend to do? How will you do it? Why is this work so important? What has already been done? Provide a brief overview of the entire proposal including the amount of grant funding you are requesting. Then, write your cover letter following the guidelines provided in Chapter 5.

We truly hope that you're finding *Winning Grants* useful. If you have feedback, whether positive or negative, please leave a review. Our goal is to provide the best possible books for you, and your reviews are crucial in achieving that.

STAGE 3: REVIEWING YOUR PROPOSAL FOR COMMON PITFALLS

8

WHY DO GRANT PROPOSALS GET REJECTED?

You send off your grant proposal and wait patiently. The days, weeks, and months pass. Eventually, you receive a response—a generic "Thank you, but..." Immediately, you enter into a tailspin and begin second-guessing everything you did. Where did you go wrong? What else could you have included? After all those hours spent crossing *t*'s and dotting *i*'s, this is a real blow.

Getting an impersonal rejection with no reasons or suggestions invariably stings. However, funders rarely provide justification for denying your request. Numbers-wise, they are forced to turn down the majority of proposals that land on their desk. It takes a lot of resources to review all those applications; they simply may not have the time or people power to respond personally to each applicant. However, there are some common reasons that cause grantmakers to reject applications. Let's examine these in more detail and wrap up with some pointers on building credibility for your nonprofit to improve your chances next time around.

MISALIGNED GOALS

This is by far the main reason most funding requests are unsuccessful. If your nonprofit's goals do not match up with the funder's goals from the very start, then your proposal will not be in the running for long. Just like your organization, a foundation, government agency, or corporation will have a particular focus when it comes to projects it chooses to fund. Ideally, there should be an obvious relationship between your project or nonprofit and the priorities of the funder you apply to. That might be synergy in terms of target population, location served, or the type of service or program being provided.

Think back and ask yourself whether you fully understood the priorities of the funding agency. On the surface, it might have seemed like your organizations shared a similar vision and were both headed in the same direction. However, perhaps the more granular objectives of your proposal were not exactly in line with their specific goals. Consider the funder's vision, mission statement, values, and the inferred outcomes of those guiding principles. It may be the case that upon closer inspection, your goals were not as closely aligned as you imagined, or perhaps your application did not highlight the relevant connections clearly enough for the reader.

YOUR NONPROFIT DID NOT SEEM READY FOR FUNDING

Another reason grant applications frequently fail comes down to organizational readiness. In other words, your organization is not ready for funding or does not appear to be ready for it. Perception is as important as reality. Start by examining your nonprofit's structure. Is it a trust, association, or corporation? Who are the key players at the top level? Do they each fill a specific role in which they have particular expertise, or are some covering multiple functions? Ideally, your leadership team should be diverse, and each member should bring a track record of success in their respective areas. Any organizational audits should be carried out by wholly independent and respected firms. Being able to demonstrate efficiency will also elevate perceptions of your organizational readiness. Some grant givers will evaluate the percentage of total expenses going toward program costs. The majority—ideally 75% and up—of your organization's expenditure should be directed toward the delivery of your programs or services.

In addition to having your financial house in good order, funders expect to see clear goals, activities, and measures. Do your vision, mission statement, and goals reflect the maturity level of your nonprofit? Are these supported by robust evidence of needs or gaps in this area? Competency and capacity to execute also go hand in hand with organizational readiness. Are your staff members capable of implementing the work outlined by your grant application and prepared to execute? Do they have the necessary skills to evaluate and document the outcomes that need to be tracked? What about managing ongoing communications and compiling regular reports?

NON-MEASURABLE PROGRAM OBJECTIVES

High on the list of common reasons for rejection is a lack of clearly articulated objectives. Have you used realistic, definitive objectives? Recall that objectives are tangible subsets of often intangible goals. Ill-defined or hard to measure objectives can be a death knell for any grant proposal. A grantmaker is naturally going to assess your plan of action in relation to the desired outcomes. It is important to determine how you will quantify the impact of your project or program. You will then need to explain the exact steps required to achieve those objectives in your application.

A WEAK BUDGET

The financial section of your grant proposal must be able to withstand scrutiny. Any anomalies will stand out to the eye of a seasoned reviewer. Grant givers are financially savvy and can quickly spot problems or inconsistencies in a proposed budget from a mile off. Be realistic and transparent with every line item. Areas like staffing or consultant costs will usually be the most closely examined. You can also expect that funders will be looking for any estimates that you may have taken liberties with, so aim for the highest degree of accuracy possible. If you do not have complete confidence in your budget, neither will an outsider.

NOT FOLLOWING INSTRUCTIONS TO THE LETTER

Most grant givers supply guidelines, if not specific instructions and templates, as to how they want applications presented. For one thing, standardized proposals are easier to review. For another, this minimizes the number of applicants blasting out a one-size-fits-all application. It also helps to weed out any nonprofits that do not follow the provided instructions. Simply ensuring you adhere to the guidelines and meet the application deadline is a non-negotiable first step. Otherwise, you will not make it to the next round for consideration. Follow the structure and format as outlined down to the smallest details. Resist the urge to include a host of supporting documentation simply because you believe it might help your chances of securing the grant.

A POORLY WRITTEN APPLICATION

If you approach grant writing with the mindset that a proposal is the equivalent of a prospectus designed to attract like-minded people to invest in your organization, you will have a head start. A grant application is your best chance to make a good impression. Make it easy to read. Write in an accessible manner that can be understood by anyone, even someone unfamiliar with your sector. Write in specifics and focus on tangible concepts wherever possible. If it takes a reviewer too long to figure out what you are trying to say, they will likely lose interest and move on to the next one. Keep your writing concise. While it may be tempting to try and pack in more detail, this will not work in your favor. Finally, any sloppy writing will obviously count against you. Proofread your work thoroughly and ask a third party to read it through with fresh eyes to ensure your proposal is polished to a high standard.

LACK OF CREDIBILITY

Nonprofits also fail to win grants because of a lack of credibility. This is especially true when you are starting out and angling for your first grant or first big donor. Grantmaking agencies want to know that their funds are being distributed to trustworthy nonprofits with integrity. You know that your mission is worthy and that your entire team takes it very seriously. You also need a track record in order to be considered credible by outside funders. One way to combat this perceived weakness is to partner with other reputable organizations that are more established, essentially piggybacking off their name by association. However, your nonprofit will also need to build its own credibility by reducing information asymmetry and cultivating an image that evokes trust.

You should aim to develop a solid communications and engagement strategy to build visibility and engender trust with your community, donors, and media. Unlike advertising, public relations is about reaching out to media and influencers to build your presence without paying for coverage. As your nonprofit's name begins to appear in more and more outlets, this will enhance trust and goodwill on the part of donors—often resulting in an increase in donations.

Using media to build credibility for your brand can have an immediate impact if you can land a mention in a mainstream publication. The media loves a feel-good story. Sometimes they may approach you, but more often than not, it will be up to you to let them know about what your organization is up to. As with engaging early with potential funders, it is worth taking a similar approach to engaging journalists. Do some research to ensure you are contacting the right reporters. You could compile a list of reporters who cover stories in your area or in your industry and follow them on Twitter or LinkedIn. Reshare or comment on their posts and follow up by pitching them a story about your cause. You must present an interesting and timely angle in order to capture their attention.

Consider where your target audience spends their time and what media they consume. The best way to reach people and get the word out about your mission is to show up where they already are. Consider reaching out to podcast hosts about setting up an interview; they are often looking for interesting guests to feature and have a dedicated audience soaking up every episode. There are a surprising number of existing podcasts in the nonprofit space. You are bound to find a few candidates. You can also reach out to relevant websites and blogs and propose writing a guest post for them. While this will obviously give you more exposure to their audience and increased brand visibility through SEO, they also stand to benefit through gaining fresh content to publish. When crafting your pitch, explain why you are approaching them specifically and how this blog post will provide value to their readers.

As with any partnership, collaborations work best when there is clear synergy between both parties' missions. For example, Mothers Against Drunk Driving partnered with Uber. Consider teaming up with other organizations or corporations to leverage their audience, customer base, or workforce. This gets your name and work in front of a new group of people. You might ask a local restaurant to donate a percentage of one day's sales to your cause or organize a raffle with a local sports team. In return, you would encourage your nonprofit's supporters to show up and spend their money there. Many workplaces are happy to support local charity projects through sponsorship, in-kind donations, and volunteer hours. This goes for local, in-person events too. Establish a presence at cultural and holiday celebrations, markets, or any other relevant events that draw crowds. You can contact event organizers and ask what role your organization could play on the day or what support you can provide.

Spend some time building your nonprofit's online presence by growing and nurturing a following on social media. The viral nature of social networks means that the more traction your content gets, the more momentum you build overall. You can also use relevant hashtags to make your content easier to discover. Be strategic in your approach and plan out what kind of content you will share, how often, and on which platforms. For example, along with sharing content about your programs and services, you can share more about each of your staff members, your organizational history, industry trends, and even amplify what your partners and sponsors are sharing on their own channels. Make the most of the visual nature of Facebook, Instagram, Pinterest, TikTok, etc. Share videos and images as much as possible. Give fans a reason to follow you. Respond to their comments, encourage tagging, and do not be afraid to use humor—people are seeking to be entertained on social media.

Finally, putting out your own content also serves to build your organization's credibility. Webinars and blog posts can then be easily repurposed into all manner of formats: syndicated to other publications, turned into infographics or SlideShare presentations, adapted into a LinkedIn column, or posted on social media. Do not try to reinvent the wheel every time. Take what you have and get more mileage out of it by molding it to suit other purposes. You should be able to reuse every piece of content in at least one other channel—one way or another.

CHAPTER ACTIVITY: REVIEW YOUR PROPOSAL AND RUN IT BY YOUR WORKING GROUP

Take time to go through your proposal to see if you have avoided the pitfalls discussed in this chapter.

- Do your goals align with your funders'? Read through their requirements one last time as you check your proposal.
- Are the goals of your project measurable?
- Is your proposal as detailed as it should be, with everything in the right place?
- Is your budget tight and reasonable?
- Have you established your credibility? Have you listed any partnerships you may have?

Have your working group go through the proposal and give feedback for each section. You can send them a list of things to look for as they review your proposal so that they catch anything that you may have missed. As they provide feedback, check your proposal against the cheat sheet in Chapter 9 as well.

9

YOUR CHECKLIST CHEAT SHEET

N ow it is time for one final run through. Before you hit the submit button, you should always cross check proposals to make sure they hit the mark and embody all the characteristics of successful grant applications. Take a moment to review your proposal against this checklist. How many of these boxes does your grant application tick?

- **Contains SMART objectives in your project description**

What exactly will your project have achieved at the end of the grant period? What might the wider impact be beyond the immediate target audience? The broader the significance of the work, the better. It is also vital to tie your project objectives back to the priorities and goals of the funder. Always articulate project objectives using the SMART framework. They should be specific, measurable, achievable, realistic, and timely.

- **Clear, concise, compelling writing**

At the macro level, ensure you have clearly articulated your organization's mission, track record, goals, projected impact, and work plan. Ensure you have provided relevant details in each section and answered the key question. Incorporate a blend of statistics and anecdotes to bring the issue to life. When done right, a reader should come away eager to act on your proposed idea

Format your proposal so that it is easy to read. Break up dense text with subheadings, paragraphs, bullet points, boxes, figures, and diagrams. Lastly, ensure you do not exceed the word limit.

- **A powerful evaluation section**

The impact evaluation section of your grant proposal should outline how you will measure outcomes, why you have selected that particular method, who is responsible for tracking these metrics, what tools they will use, and when they will do so. This does not automatically require external evaluators or the use of new tools or methods. Consider how your nonprofit currently collects and analyzes data. There is no need to reinvent the wheel unnecessarily.

- **A well-crafted, thoughtful submission that has been reviewed by a colleague**

There is no excuse for cutting corners and dashing off a hastily put-together application. Take care to present information in a logical fashion, including facts and numbers that support a thorough and compelling proposal. Your work plan should address specific activities, accountability, timelines, and partnerships.

While it may read well to you, you are too close to the work to conduct the final review. Your brain and eyes start to read what should be there, rather than what is actually there. That is why you need an outsider to read through your submission well before the deadline. Enlist a trusted colleague to give feedback on your proposal, not only in terms of spelling and grammar, but to check whether your overall writing style is succinct and compelling. You may find that they spot gaps in the supporting details where you have not thoroughly answered the question at hand.

- **Shows passion specific to the topic/field**

Passion is an essential ingredient in any grant proposal. Your nonprofit's mission and story come into play here. Do not be afraid to highlight the origin story that led to its founding. A strong "why" is what keeps charitable causes going despite the many challenges they face. In your grant proposal, focus on opportunities, rather than hurdles or problems. Stress the unique qualities of your project and organization, while demonstrating a broad knowledge of similar initiatives in the wider sector.

- **Builds on your organization's track record**

Your grant application should place your proposed project or program within the overall context of your nonprofit's mission. Craft a punchy cover letter that presents an overview of your organization and your project, and relevant background material to support this narrative. It is crucial to present your nonprofit's history in the best possible light, showing how it is qualified to deliver the work ahead. Pointing to your established track record of success will give a funder confidence in your capacity to continue in the same vein. If your nonprofit is young and lacking sufficient experience in the field, play up other evidence of its credibility, such as media coverage and partnerships with established organizations.

If you have made it this far, congratulations! You are officially ready to send your grant proposal and take the next step toward winning more funding for your non-profit organization—preparing other proposals. All you need to do is clean it up and submit it to your top prospect.

CHAPTER ACTIVITY: CLEAN IT UP, PACKAGE IT AND HIT SEND

Give your proposal to a colleague you trust or perform the final clean up yourself. If you choose to do it yourself, give yourself a day or two to step away from the proposal and do other things. That way, when you come back to it, you will see it with fresh eyes. Check to see that the message is as clear as possible and evaluate the effect it is likely to have on the reader. Is the effect what you desired? Is your purpose clear? Is there irrelevant information? Are the ideas clear? Are your data/examples accurate? Is the tone appropriate for your audience? Is the length optimal?

Edit the structure as well. Does the proposal look appealing? See if the structure is organized; ensure that ideas flow logically and each section is at the right place. Is there a clear executive summary? Are there enough paragraphs? Does each paragraph have a clear topic sentence? Have you linked the sentences well? Make sure that the language you use is grammatically correct and remember to spell check. Use appropriate vocabulary and punctuation. Grammarly is very helpful with this—editing and proofreading.

The final thing to check for at this stage is the formatting. Good writing includes high readability. Does your final product look good? What font have you chosen? Have you highlighted important ideas? Is the formatting consistent? If you have done the previous steps well, this last one should take you ten minutes or less depending on the length of your proposal. You normally review to make sure that your content reads well and that the final draft has the intended effect on the reader. If possible, read parts of your writing aloud and listen to how they sound.

Remember that part of cleaning up your grant proposal is attaching any required additional documents. Add an appendices section with your budget and any extra material that makes it easier for the funder to understand your situation and appreciate your solution. Where possible, use charts and tables to illustrate ideas rather than simply describing them with words alone. Once you have done all this, your proposal is ready to be submitted. Submit it through the proper channels. All the best with your proposal!

FINAL THOUGHTS

If your nonprofit is in a tight spot and looking to raise funds quickly, grants are unlikely to be the silver bullet for your organization. However, they are a great solution for charities seeking funds to deliver pre-planned programs and should make up part of your long-term revenue strategy. Nonprofits must maintain diverse streams of income to reduce risk and ensure sustainability. Grant funding can play a key role in funding growth and launching new programs that otherwise wouldn't be possible. Receiving a grant from a well-respected foundation or government agency can also boost your organization's credibility. This in turn can help you land even more funding from other sources going forward. There are billions of dollars' worth of grants out there offered by foundations, government agencies, corporations, and other grantmakers. According to Grant Station (2019), the median largest individual award for grant seekers that year was $69,100. There are grants available for all kinds and sizes of nonprofits, and while many are designed to fund specific projects, there are also plenty that will help to cover operating expenses or capital costs.

That said, this money is not just sitting around waiting to be claimed. You will need to put in the work to ensure you meet the criteria and craft a compelling case for why your nonprofit deserves to receive its share of the pot. It does not end there, either—once funds are awarded, it is up to you to deliver on what was promised and report back on the impact of your project or program.

Remember that every grant-giving organization will have different requirements. Your success hinges largely on finding a suitable match and then crafting a narrative that connects with those values and pitches your nonprofit as a natural partner. No matter how powerful your nonprofit's mission, if you cannot tell a compelling story that weaves together its vision and impact, you will struggle to win attention and funding. The most successful grant recipients understand this and apply these core principles to every application sent out.

Developing grant writing skills is an invaluable asset for any nonprofit professional. Once you know how to write and win grant proposals, this can become a dependable source of revenue. Fortunately, following some best practices for writing grant proposals will set you ahead of the pack from the get-go.

By now, you should have a firm grasp of nonprofit grants, how to find potential opportunities, and how to engage with a funder early on to improve your chances of success. Throughout this book, I have walked you through the steps involved in writing an irresistible grant application—breaking down the elements of a proposal with specific examples and providing activities for you to do toward finishing a grant proposal. Finally, I outlined some common mistakes that frequently result in rejection and provided a cheat sheet to check your proposal against. You can refer back to that section before sending off each application to ensure it stands out and avoids the most common pitfalls that plague grant writers.

My vision in writing this book was to alleviate any apprehension you may feel in relation to grant writing and equip you with the confidence and insider knowledge to succeed. Now that you have the tools, go forth and win your next proposal!

We truly hope that you've gained a lot from *Winning Grants*. Our goal is to provide as much value for you as possible and we hope we were able to achieve that. If you have feedback for the author, whether positive or negative, we'd love it if you left a review.

To leave a review, go to:
Amazon.com/review/create-review?
&asin=B09YYMVHRY

Or scan with your camera:

REFERENCES

Bridgespan. (2011.) Donors want more information on impact.
https://www.bridgespan.org/insights/blog/measuring-to-improve/blog-donors-want-more-information-on-impact

Candid. (2020.) Key facts on U.S. non-profits and foundations.
https://www.issuelab.org/resources/36381/36381.pdf

Charity: water. (2022.) About Us | charity: water.
https://www.charitywater.org/uk/about

Deloitte. (2015.) Case studies in funding innovation.
https://www2.deloitte.com/content/dam/insights/us/

articles/case-studies-in-funding-innovation-gates-foundation-grand-challenges-explorations/Funding-innovation_ENTIRE-ARTICLE_vFINAL_10_15_15.pdf

Engineers Without Borders. (2017.) 2017 Failure Report. https://www.ewb.ca/wp-content/uploads/2018/08/EWB_FAILURE-REPORT_EN_03-08-2018-pages.pdf

European Venture Philanthropy Association. (2015.) Learning from failures in venture philanthropy and social investment. https://evpa.eu.com/uploads/publications/Learning-from-failures_EVPA_2015report.pdf

Fidelity. (2016.) The future of philanthropy. https://www.fidelitycharitable.org/content/dam/fc-public/docs/insights/the-future-of-philanthropy.pdf

Fidelity. (2017.) Fidelity charitable study finds 64% of donors want to give more to charity, concerned about personal finances and impact. https://www.fidelitycharitable.org/about-us/news/study-finds-64-percent-of-donors-want-to-give-more.html

First Descents. (2022.) Who We Are - First Descents.
https://firstdescents.org/who-we-are/

Foundation Center. (2004.) Foundation growth and
giving estimates, 2004 preview.
https://www.issuelab.org/resources/24885/24885.pdf

GrantStation. (2019.) The 2019 state of grantseeking
report.
https://grantstation.com/sites/default/files/2019-05/
The%202019%20State%20of%20Grantseeking%
20Report_0.pdf

Harvard Business Review. (2010.) The emerging capital
market for non-profits.
https://hbr.org/2010/10/the-emerging-capital-
market-for-nonprofits

Harvard Business Review. (1997.) Virtuous capital:
what foundations can learn from venture capitalists.
https://hbr.org/1997/03/virtuous-capital-what-founda
tions-can-learn-from-venture-capitalists

King, Bernard J. (2011.) Poverty and literacy development: challenges for global educators.
https://core.ac.uk/download/pdf/11049014.pdf

National Philanthropic Trust. Charitable giving statistics.
https://www.nptrust.org/philanthropic-resources/charitable-giving-statistics/
and
https://www.nptuk.org/philanthropic-resources/uk-charitable-giving-statistics/

New York Times. (2012.) Getting into a benefactor's head.
https://www.nytimes.com/2012/11/09/giving/understanding-donor-behavior-to-increase-contributions.html

OECD. (2013.) England & Northern Ireland (UK) – Country Note –Survey of Adult Skills first results.
https://www.oecd.org/skills/piaac/Country%20note%20-%20United%20Kingdom.pdf

Stanford Social Innovation Review. (2007.) How non-profits get really big.
https://ssir.org/articles/entry/how_non-profits_get_really_big#

Submittable. (2020.) 34 grant statistics for 2020.
https://blog.submittable.com/grant-statistics/

The Annie E. Casey Foundation. (2004.) Moving youth from risk to opportunity.
https://files.eric.ed.gov/fulltext/ED485937.pdf

The Guardian. (2015.) Proving your impact: what funders want from charities.
https://www.theguardian.com/society-professionals/2015/nov/04/impact-funders-charities-foundations-measurement

Watts of Love. (2021.) Our Values - Watts of Love.
https://www.wattsoflove.org/about/our-values

Made in the USA
Las Vegas, NV
09 July 2023

74416968R00121